SOLUTIONS MANUAL

to accompany

INVESTMENTS

Second Edition

Zvi Bodie
Boston University

Alex Kane
University of California, San Diego

Alan Marcus
Boston College

IRWIN
Burr Ridge, Illinois
Boston, Massachusetts
Sydney, Australia

ISBN 0-256-14401-X

1 1 P 0 9 8 7 6 5

CHAPTER 1 : THE INVESTMENT ENVIRONMENT

1. a. Cash is a financial asset because it is the liability of the government.
   b. No.
   c. Yes.
   d. The tax payers as a group will make up for the liability.

2. The ratio is .029 for financial institutions, and .77 for the non-financial business sector. The difference should be expected mainly because the bulk of the business of financial institutions is to make loans which are financial assets.

3. The tax increased the relative value of Eurobonds, contributing to the growth of that market.

4. a. Primary-market transaction
   b. Derivative security.
   c. Investors who wish to hold gold without the complication of physical storage.

5. Securitization requires access to a large number of potential investors. To attract them the capital market needs: 1) a safe system of business laws and low probability of confiscatory taxation/regulation, 2) a well developed investment banking industry, 3) a well developed system of brokerage and financial transactions, and 4) a well developed media, particularly financial reporting. These are found (indeed make) a well developed financial market.

6. a. No. Diversification calls for investing your savings in assets that do well when GM is doing poorly.

   b. No. Although Toyota is a competitor of GM, both are subject to fluctuations in the automobile market.

7. Unlike fixed salary contracts, bonuses create better incentives for executives.

8. Securitization is the mechanism for disintermediation. Financial intermediaries must increase other activities such as providing short-term liquidity to consumers and small business, and financial services.

9. Contraction of the supply of financial assets would make financing more difficult, increasing the cost of capital. A higher cost of capital means less investment and lower real growth.

10. A pool of third-world debt may include $10 billion allocated $1 billion each to 10 governments that are considered of equal default risk. Each government amortizes its debt in equal payments over 15 years. Shares in the cashflows from the package are then sold to investors.

11. Due to the elements and pests, farming is riskier than the manufacturing of pencils or paper. Therefore, farmers have a greater demand for hedging.

CHAPTER 2 : MARKETS AND INSTRUMENTS

1. a. (iv)
    b. (iii)

2. a. $r_{BEY} = \dfrac{(10,000 - P)}{P} \times \dfrac{365}{n}$

    $= \dfrac{10000 - 9600}{9600} \times \dfrac{365}{180} = 08449$, or 8.45%

    b. One reason is that the discount yield is computed by dividing the dollar discount from par by the par value, \$10,000, rather than by the bill's price, \$9,600. A second reason is that the discount yield is annualized by a 360-day year rather than 365.

3. $P = 10,000\ [1 - d\ (n/360)]$ where d is the discount yield.
    $P_{ask} = 10,000\ [1 - .0681\ (60/360)] = \$9,886.50$
    $P_{bid} = 10,000\ [1 - .0690\ (60/360)] = \$9,885.00$

4. $r_{BEY} = \dfrac{(10,000 - P)}{P} \times \dfrac{365}{n}$

    $= \dfrac{10000 - 9886.50}{9886.50} \times \dfrac{365}{n} = 6.98\%,$

    which exceeds 6.81%.

5. a. i. $1 + r = (10,000/9,764)^4 = 1.100$
            $r = 10\%$

    ii. $1 + r = (10,000/9,539)^2 = 1.099$
            $r = 9.9\%$

    The three-month bill offers a higher effective annual yield.

    b. i. $r_{BD} = \dfrac{10000 - 9764}{10000} \times \dfrac{360}{91} = .0934$

    ii. $r_{BD} = \dfrac{10000 - 9539}{10000} \times \dfrac{360}{91} = .0912$

6. The total before-tax income is \$4, of which .20 x \$4 = \$.80 is taxable income (after the 80% exclusion). Taxes therefore are .30 x \$.80 = \$.24, for an after-tax income of \$3.76, and a rate of return of 9.4%.

7. a. The index at t=0 is (90 + 50 + 100)/3 = 80. At t=l, it is 250/3 = 83.33, for a rate of return of 4.167%.

    b. In the absence of a split, stock C would sell for 110, and the index would be 250/3 = 83.33. After the split, stock C sells at 55. Therefore, we need to set the divisor d such that 83.33 = (95 + 45 + 55)/d, meaning that d = 2.34.

c. The return is zero. The index remains unchanged, as it should, since the return on each stock separately equals zero.

8. a. Total market value at t=0 is (9,000 + 10,000 + 20,000) = 39,000. Market value at t=1 is (9,500 + 9,000 + 22,000) = 40,500. Rate of return = 40,500/39,000 - 1 = 3.85%.

b. The return on each stock is as follows:

$$r_A = 95/90 - 1 = .0556$$
$$r_B = 45/50 - 1 = -.10$$
$$r_C = 110/100 - 1 = .10$$

The equally-weighted average is .0185 = 1.85%

c. The geometric average return is $[(1.0556)(.9)(1.10)]^{1/3} - 1 = .0148 = 1.48\%$.

9. The after-tax yield on the corporate bonds is .09(1 - .28) = .0648. Therefore, munis must pay at least 6.48%.

10. a. The taxable bond. The after tax rate is still 5 percent.
   b. The taxable bond. Its after tax rate is 5(1 - .1) = 4.5%
   c. You are indifferent.
   d. The muni.

11. Equation (2.5) shows that the equivalent taxable yield is: $r = r_m/(1 - t)$.
   a. 4%
   b. 4.4%
   c. 5%
   d. 5.71%

12. a. The higher coupon bond.
   b. The call with the lower exercise price.
   c. The put on the lower priced stock.
   d. The bill with the lower yield.

13. There is always a chance that the option will expire in the money. Investors will pay something for this chance of a positive payoff.

14.

	Value of call at expiration	-	Initial Cost	=	Profit
a.	0		4		-4
b.	0		4		-4
c.	0		4		-4
d.	5		4		1
e.	10		4		6

	Value of put at expiration	-	Initial Cost	=	Profit
a.	10		64		4
b.	5		6		-1
c.	0		6		-6
d.	0		6		-6
e.	0		6		-6

15. The put option conveys the __right__ to sell the asset at the exercise price. The short futures contract carries an __obligation__ to sell it for the futures price.

16. The call option conveys the __right__ to buy the asset at the exercise price. The long futures contract carries an __obligation__ to buy it for the futures price.

17. The spead will widen. A deterioration in the economy increases enterpise risk of default.

18. 22 of the 25 stocks meet this criterion, leading us to conclude that returns on stock investments can be quite volatile.

CHAPTER 3 : HOW SECURITIES ARE TRADED

1. a. In addition to the explicit fees of $70,000, FBN appears to have paid an implicit price in underpricing of the IPO. The underpricing is $3/share or $300,000 total, implying total costs of $370,000.

   b. No. The underwriters do not capture the part of the costs corresponding to the underpricing. The underpricing may be a rational marketing strategy. Without it, the underwriters would need to spend more resources to place the issue with the public. They would then need to charge higher explicit fees to the issuing firm. The issuing firm may be just as well off paying the implicit issuance cost represented by the underpricing.

2. a. In principle, potential losses are unbounded, growing directly with increases in the price of IBM.

   b. If the stop-buy order can be filled at $128, the maximum possible loss per share is $8. If IBM shares go above $128, the stop-buy order is executed, limiting the losses from the short sale.

3. The limit-sell order will be exercised as soon as the stock price hits the limit price. If the stock price later rebounds, the investor does not participate in the gains because the stock has been sold. In contrast, the put option need not be exercised when the stock price falls below the exercise price. An investor who owns a share of stock and a put option can hold on to both securities. If the stock price never rebounds, the put eventually can be exercised, and the stock sold for the exercise price. This provides the same downside protection as the limit-sell order. If the price does rebound, however, the investor benefits because the stock is still held. This advantage of the put over the limit-sell order justifies the cost of the put.

4. Calls give the option to purchase a stock at any time prior to expiration. Limit-buys require purchase as soon as the stock price hits the limit. The advantage of the call over the limit-buy is that the investor need not commit to buying until expiration. If the stock price later falls, the holder of the call can choose not to purchase.

5. The broker is to attempt to sell Marriott as soon as the stock was sold at a bid price of 38 or less. Here, the broker will attempt to execute.

6. Much of what the specialist does--crossing orders and maintaining the limit order book-- can be accomplished by a computerized system. In fact, some exchanges use an automated system for night trading. A more difficult issue is whether the more discretionary activities of specialists that involve trading for their own accounts, such as maintaining an orderly market, can be replicated by a computer system.

7. a. The buy order will be filled at the best limit-sell order, $50.25.

   b. At the next-best price, $51.50.

   c. You should increase your position. There is considerable buy pressure at prices just below $50, meaning that downside risk is limited. In contrast, sell pressure is sparse, meaning that a moderate buy order could result in a substantial price increase.

8. The system expedites the flow of orders from exchange members to the specialists. It

allows members to send computerized orders, necessary for program trading.

9. The dealer.
    Spread should be higher on inactive stocks and lower on active stocks.

10.a. Generally, the price of a seat increases as trading volume increases.

  b. Increase in volume and return to scale suggest a decrease in competitive commissions.

11.a. You buy 200 shares in AT&T. These shares increase in value by 10%, or $1,000. You pay interest of .08 x 5,000 = $400. The rate of return will be

$$\frac{1000 - 400}{5000} = .12, \text{ or } 12\%.$$

  b. The value of the 200 shares is 200P. Equity is 200P - 5,000. You will receive a margin call when

$$\frac{200P - 5000}{200P} = .30 \quad \text{or when } P = \$35.71.$$

12.a. You will not receive a margin call. You borrowed $20,000 and with $20,000 of equity you bought 500 share of Disney at $80 a share. At $75 a share the market value of the account is $37,500, your equity is $17,500, and the margin rate is 47%.

  b. As shown in section 3.6 page 98, the price for a maintenance margin call is $53.33.

13.a. Initial margin is 50% of $5,000 or $2,500.

  b. Total assets are $7,500, and liabilities are lOOP. A margin call will be issued when

$$\frac{7500 - 100P}{100P} = .3 \quad \text{or when } P = \$57.69.$$

14. The proceeds from the short sale was 14x100 - 50 = $1,350. Assuming m =.5 you must deposit $700. A dividend payment of $200 was withdrawn from the account, leaving in the account $1,850. Coverage at $9 cost you 900+50=$950., leaving you with $1,000 and a profit of $200. Note that $200 = 100 (14- 9 - 2 - 2x.5)

16. (d) The broker will attempt to sell after the first transaction at $55 or less.

17. (b)

18. (d)

CHAPTER 4 : CONCEPTS AND ISSUES

1.   Your holding period return for the next year on the money market fund depends on what 30 day interest rates will be each month when it is time to roll over maturing securities. The one-year savings deposit will offer a 7.5% HPR for the year. If you forecast the rate on money market instruments to rise significantly above the current yield of 6%, then the money market fund might result in a higher HPR for the year. While the 20-year Treasury bond is offering a yield to maturity of 9% per year, which is 150 basis points higher than the rate on the one-year savings deposit at the bank, you could wind up with a one-year HP of much less than 7.5% on the bond if long-term interest rates rise during the year. If Treasury bond yields rise above 9% during the year, then the price of the bond will fall, and the capital loss will wipe out some or all of the 9% yield you would have received if bond yields had remained the same as they were at the beginning of the year.

2. a.   If businesses increase their capital spending they are likely to increase their demand for funds. This will shift the demand curve in Figure 4.1 to the right and increase the equilibrium real rate of interest.

   b.   Increased household saving will shift the supply curve to the right and cause real interest rates to fall.

   c.   An open market sale of Treasury securities by the Fed is equivalent to a reduction in the supply of funds (a shift of the supply curve to the left) or an increase in the demand for funds (a shift of the demand curve to the right). Either way you look at it, the equilibrium real rate of interest will rise.

3. a.   The Inflation-Plus CD is safer because it guarantees the purchasing power of the investment.

   b.   The expected return depends on the rate of inflation over the next year. If the rate of inflation is less than 5% then the conventional CD will offer a higher real return than the Inflation-Plus CD; if inflation is more than 5%, the opposite will be true.

   c.   If you expect the rate of inflation to be 4% over the next year, then the conventional CD offers you an expected real rate of return of 4%, which is 1% higher than the real rate on the IP CD. But unless you know that inflation will be 4% with certainty, the conventional CD is also riskier. The question of which is the better investment then depends on your attitude towards risk vs. return. You would probably want to diversify and invest part of your funds in each.

   d.   No. We cannot infer that the entire difference between the normal risk-free rate (on conventional CDs) of 8% and the real risk-free rate (on IP CDs) of 3% is the expected rate of inflation. Part of the difference is probably a real risk premium on the conventional CDs. This implies that the expected rate of inflation is less than 5% per year.

4. $E(r)$ $= .3 \times 44\% + .4 \times 14\% + .3 \times (-16\%) = 14\%$.

          Variance $= .3 \times (44 - 14)^2 + .4 \times (14 - 14)^2 + .3 \times (-16 - 14)^2 = 540$

          Standard deviation $= 23.24\%$

   The mean is unchanged, but the standard deviation has gone up.

5. Probability Distribution of Price and 1-Year HPR on 30-year Treasuries

State of the Economy	Probability	YTM	Price	HPR
Boom	.25	12%	75.93	-15.07%
Normal Growth	.50	.9	100	9%
Recession	.25	7.5	117.54	26.54%

6. The average risk premium on stocks for the period 1926-1990 is 8.40% per year. Adding this to a risk-free rate of 8% gives an E(r) of 16.40% per year for the S&P 500 portfolio.

7. The average risk premiums and standard deviation are very different in the sub periods:

	STOCKS		BONDS	
	Mean	Std. Dev.	Mean	Std. Dev.
1926-1990	8.40%	21.10%	1.17%	8.31%
1961-1990	4.79	16.10	.14	10.62
1926-1941	6.00	29.56	3.58	5.24

I would prefer to use the risk premiums and standard deviations estimated over the period 1961-1990, because it seems to have been a different economic regime. After 1955 the U.S. economy entered the Post-Keynesian era, when the Federal government assumed responsibility for stabilizing the economy and preventing extreme cycles of boom and bust. Note that the standard deviation of stocks has gone down in the later period while the standard deviation of bonds has gone up.

8. a Real HPR = (1 + Nominal HPR)/(1 + Inflation)-1
     = (Nominal HPR - Inflation)/(1 + Inflation) = (.8 - .7)/1.7 = .0588 or 5.88%

   b. The approximation gives a real HPR of 10%, which is clearly too high.

9. Probability Distribution of HPR on Insurance Policy

Scenario	Probability	HPR on Insurance Policy
Fire	.001	49,900%
No fire	.999	-100%

   a. E(r) = -50%

   b. Standard deviation = 1,580%

   c. The policy is not risky because when combined with the house it reduces your overall risk.

10. From Table 4.2, average real rates are, approximately, 3.73 - 3.25 = .48% for bills, and 8.88% for stocks.

   a. 3.48%

b. 11.88%

c. The risk premium on stocks remains unchanged. [A premium, the difference between two rates, is real].

11. Real interest rates are expected to rise.

12. Possibly. A risky stock could provide a hedge against a specific risk.

13.a. Probability Distribution of HPR on the Stock Market and Put

State of the Economy	Probability	Stock Ending Price	HPR	Put Ending Value	HPR
Boom	.25	$140	44%	0	-100%
Normal Growth	.50	110	14%	0	-100%
Recession	.25	80	-16%	$30	150%

Remember that the cost of the stock is $100 per share, and that of the put is $12.

b. The cost of one share of stock plus a put is $112. The Probability Distribution of HPR on the Stock Market plus Put is:

State of the Economy	Probability	Stock Plus Put Ending Value	HPR	
Boom	.25	$144	28.6%	(144 - 112)/112
Normal Growth	.50	114	1.8%	(114 - 112)/112
Recession	.25	114	1.8%	

c. Buying the put option guarantees you a minimum HPR of 1.8% regardless of what happens to the stock's price. Thus it is insurance against a price decline.

d. If the market price of the put option were less than $10 when the stock's price is $100, it would pay to buy the put option and a share of stock and exercise it immediately for a risk-free arbitrage profit. For example, if the put's price were $9, you would simultaneously buy a put and a share of stock for a total cost of $109 and then exercise the put and receive $110 for your share of stock. There would be an immediate profit of $1. Since many market participants are constantly looking for arbitrage opportunities like this, their attempts to buy such an underpriced put would drive its price up until the arbitrage opportunity disappears.

14.a. Probability Distribution of Dollar Return on CD plus Call

State of the Economy	Probability	CD Ending Value	Call Ending Value	Combined Value
Boom	.25	$114	$30	$144
Normal Growth	.50	114	0	114
Recession	.25	114	0	114

b. Since the probability distribution of the dollar return on the call plus the CD is identical to that of the stock plus the put, they must cost the same:

Price of call $+ \dfrac{\$114}{1.06} =$ Price of put + price of stock = $112

Price of call $= \$112 - \dfrac{114}{1.06} = \$4.45$

This relationship is known as the Put-Call Parity Relationship.

CHAPTER 5 : RISK AND RISK AVERSION

1. a. The expected cash flow is: .5 x 50,000 + .5 x 150,000 = $100,000. With a risk premium of 10%, the required rate of return is 15%. Therefore, if the value of the portfolio is X, then to earn 15% expected return,

$$X(1 + .15) = 100,000,$$

implying that $\qquad$ X = $86,957.

   b. If the portfolio is purchased at $86,957, and promises an expected payoff of $100,000, then the expected rate of return, E(r), is derived as follows:

$$86,957[1 + E(r)] = 100,000$$

so that E(r) = .15. The portfolio price is set to equate the expected return with the required rate of return.

   c. If the risk premium over bills is now 15%, then the required return is 5 + 15 = 20%. The value of the portfolio, X, must satisfy: (1 + .20) = 100, 000, so X = $83,333.

   d. For a given expected cash flow, portfolios that command greater risk premia must sell at lower prices. The extra discount from expected value is penalty for risk.

2. When we specify utility by $U = E(r) - .5A\sigma^2$, the utility from bills is .08, while that from the risky portfolio is $U = .10 - .5 \times A \times .15^2 = .10 - .01125A$. For the portfolio to be preferred to bills, the following inequality must hold: .1 - .01125A > .08, or, A < -.02/(-.01125) = 1.778. A must be less than 1.778 or else the investor's risk aversion will be large enough for her to prefer bills.

3. Points on the curve are derived as follows:

$$U = .5 = E(r) - .5 \times A \times \sigma^2 = E(r) - 1.5\sigma^2$$

The necessary value of E(r), given the value of σ^2, is therefore:

$$E(r) = .05 + 1.5\sigma^2.$$

σ	σ^2	E(r)
.05	0025	.05375
.1	01	.065
.15	0225	.08375
.2	04	.11
.25	0625	.14375

The indifference curve is depicted by the solid line in the graph below.

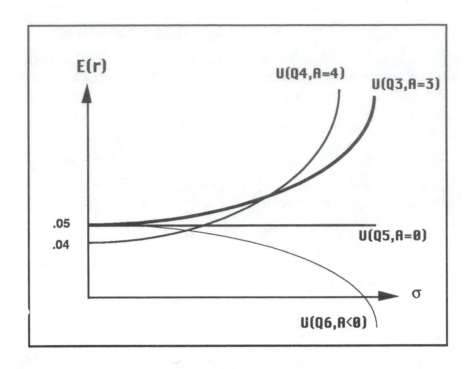

4.   Repeating the process from Problem 3, the expected return variance equation is:

$$E(r) = .04 + 2\sigma^2$$

leading to the expected return-standard deviation table below. The curve is the upward sloping dashed line in the graph of Problem 3.

σ	σ^2	$E(r)$
.05	.0025	.045
.1	.01	.06
.15	.0225	.085
.2	.04	.12
.25	.0625	.165

The indifference curve in Problem 4 differs from that in Problem 3 in both slope and intercept. When A is changed from 3 to 4 , the increase in risk aversion results in a greater slope of the indifference curve since more $E(r)$ is needed to compensate for additional σ. The lower level of utility , from .05 to .04, shifts the indifference curve downwards by .01.

5.   The coefficient of risk aversion of a risk neutral investor is zero. The corresponding utility is simply equal to the portfolio expected return. The corresponding indifference curve in the expected return-standard deviation plane is a horizontal line, as drawn in the graph of Problem 3.

6.   A risk lover, rather then penalizing a portfolio utility to account for risk, rewards its utility

in proportion to its variance. This amounts to a negative coefficient of risk aversion. The corresponding indifference curve is downward sloping, as drawn in the graph of Problem 3.

7. The portfolio expected return can be decomposed to the contributions of bills and stocks:

W_{bills}	Contribution to Rate of Return	W_{market}	Contribution to Rate of Return	Portfolio Expected Return
0.	0.	1.0	.145	.145
.2	.012	.8	.116	.128
.4	.024	.6	.087	.111
.6	.036	.4	.058	.094
.8	.048	.2	.029	.077
1.0	.06	0.	0.	.06

8. Computing the utility from $U = E(r) - 1.5\sigma^2$, (A=3), we arrive at the table below.

W_{Bills}	W_{Market}	$E(r)$	σ	σ^2	(A=3)	$U(A=5)$
0.	1.0	.145	.21	.0441	.07885	.03475
.2	.8	.128	.168	.028224	.085664	.05744
.4	.6	.111	.126	.015876	.087186	.07131
.6	.4	.094	.084	.007056	.083416	.07636
.8	.2	.077	.042	.001764	.074354	.07259
1.0	0.	.06	0.	0.	.06	.06

The utility column suggests that investors with A=3 prefer a position of 60% in the market and 40% in bills, over any of the other positions in the table.

9. The column of U(A=5) is computed from $U = E(r) - 2.5\sigma^2$. It shows that the more risk averse investor prefers the position with 40% in the market index portfolio, rather than 60% that the investor with A = 3 does.

10. The entire probability distribution is now:

	Normal Sugar Crop		Sugar Crisis
	Bullish Stock Market	Bearish Stock Market	
Probability	.5	.3	.2
Stock			
Best Candy	.25	.10	-.25
SugarKane	.10	-.05	.20
Humanex's Portfolio	.175	.025	-.025

Using the portfolio rate of return distribution, its expected return and standard deviation can be calculated as follows:

$$E(r_p) = .5 \times .175 + .3 \times .025 \times (-.025) = .09$$

$$\sigma_p = [.5(.175 - .09)^2 + .3(.025 - .09)^2 + .2(-.025 - .09)2]^{1/2} = .0867$$

11. The expected return of Best is .105 and its standard deviation .189. The mean and standard deviation of SugarKane are now:

$$E(r_{SK}) = .5 \times .10 + .3 \times (-.05) + .2 \times .20 = .075$$

$$\sigma_{SK} = [.5(.10 - .075)^2 - .3(-.05 - .075)^2 + .2(.20 - .075)^2]^{1/2} = .0901$$

and its covariance with Best is

$$\text{Cov} = .5 (.10 - .075)(.25 - .105) + .3(-.05 - .075)(.10 - .105)$$
$$+ .2(.20 - .075)(-.25 - .105) = -.006875$$

12. From the calculations in (11), the portfolio expected rate of return is

$$E(r_p) = .5 \times .105 + .5 \times .075 = .09$$

Using the portfolio weights $w_B = w_{SK} = .5$ and the covariance between the stocks, we can compute the portfolio standard deviation from rule 5.

$$\sigma_p = [w_B^2 \times \sigma_B^2 + w_{SK}^2 \times \sigma_{SK}^2 + 2 \times w_B \times w_{SK} \times \text{Cov(B,SK)}]^{1/2}$$

$$[.5^2 \times .189^2 + .5^2 \times .091^2 + 2 \times .5 \times .5 \times(-.06875)]^{1/2} = .0867$$

CHAPTER 5 : APPENDIX A

1. The current price of Klink stock is $12. Thus, the rates of return in each scenario and their deviations from the mean are given by:

Probability	Rate of Return	Deviation from the Mean
.10	-1.0000	-1.0752
.20	-.8125	-.8877
.40	.2000	.1248
.25	.7167	.6415
.05	1.5708	1.4956
1.00	Mean = .0752	
	SD = .7030	

a. Mean = .0752

Median = .20
Mode = .20

b. Std. Dev.=.7030
    MAD = Pr(i) Abs[r(i) - r] = .5701

c. The first moment is the mean (.20752), the second moment around the mean is the variance
    (.7030 - .494209) and the third is:

$$M3 = Pr(i)\ [r(i) - r]^3 = -.03015782$$

Therefore the probability distribution is negatively (left) skewed.

CHAPTER 5 : APPENDIX B

1. Your $50,000 investment will grow to $50,000(1.06) = $53,000 by year end. <u>Without
    insurance</u> your wealth will then be:

no fire:	prob.	.999	wealth	$253,000
fire:	prob.	.001	wealth	$ 53,000

    which gives expected utility

    $$.001\ X\ log_e(53,000) + .999\ X\ log_e(253,000) = 12.439582$$

    and a certainty equivalent wealth of

    $$exp(12.439582) = \$252,604.85$$

    <u>With <u>fire</u> insurance</u> at a cost of $P, your investment in the risk-free asset will be only
    $(50,000 - P). Your wealth at year end will be <u>certain</u> (since you are fully insured) and
    equal to

    $$(50,000 - P)1.06 + 200,000.$$

    Setting this expression equal to $252,604.85 (certainty equivalent of the uninsured house)
    results in P = $372.79. This is the most you will be willing to pay for insurance. Note that
    the expected loss is "only" $200, meaning that you are willing to pay quite a risk premium.
    The main reason is that the value of the house is a large proportion of your wealth.

2. a. With 1/2 coverage, your premium is $100, your investment in the safe asset is $49,900
    which grows by year end to $52,894. If there is a fire, your insurance proceeds are only
    $100,000. Your outcome will be:

Event	Prob.	Wealth
fire	.001	$152,894
no fire	.999	$252,894

    Expected utility is

$$.001 \times \log_e(152,894) + .999 \times \log_e(252,894) = 12.440222$$

and $W_{CE} = \exp(12.440222) = \$252\ 766$

b. With full coverage, costing \$200, end-of-year wealth is certain, and equal to

$$(50,000 - 200)1.06 + 200,000 = \$252,788$$

Since wealth is certain, this is also certainty equivalent wealth of the exactly insured position.

With over-insurance, the insurance costs \$300, and pays off \$300,000 in the event of a fire. The outcomes are

Event	Prob	Wealth
fire	.001	$\$352,682 = (50,000 - 300) \times 1.06 + 300,000$
no fire	.999	$\$252,682 = (50,000 - 300) \times 1.06 + 200,000$

Expected utility is

$$.001 \times \log_e(352,682) + .999 \times \log_e(252,682) = 12.4402205$$

and $\quad W_{CE} = \exp(12.4402205) = 252,766$

Therefore, full insurance dominates both over- and under-insurance. Note that over-insuring creates a gamble (you gain when, with a small probability, the house burns down, and you pay for it more than the expected gain). In moving from 50% insured to 150% insured, the utility loss from the extra 50% gamble offsets the utility gain from the additional 50% of coverage. Over-insurance is disallowed because of the moral hazard that it creates.

CHAPTER 6: CAPITAL ALLOCATION BETWEEN THE RISKY ASSET AND THE RISK-FREE ASSET

1. Mean $= .3 \times .07 + .7 \times .17 = .14$ or 14% per year.
    Standard deviation $= .7 \times .27 = .189$ or 18.9% per year

2. Investment proportions: 30% in T-bills; $.7 \times 27\% = 18.9\%$ in stock A
    $.7 \times 33\% = 23.1\%$ in stock B
    $.7 \times 40\% = 28.0\%$ in stock C

3. Reward-to-variability ratio $= \dfrac{.17 - .07}{.27} = .3704$

4.

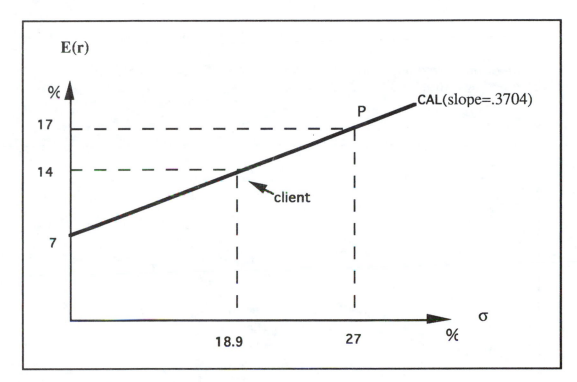

5. a. Mean of portfolio $= r_f + (r_p - r_f)y = .07 + .1y$

    If the mean of the portfolio is equal to 15% then solving for y we get:

    $.15 = .07 + .10y$ and $y = \dfrac{.15 - .07}{.10} = .8$

    So to get a mean of 15% the client must invest 80% of his funds in the risky portfolio and 20% in T-bills.

    b. Investment proportions of clients own funds:
        20% in T-bills,
        $.8 \times .27 = 21.6\%$ in stock A

$$.8 \times .33 = 26.4\% \text{ in stock B}$$
$$.8 \times .40 = 32.0\% \text{ in stock C}$$

c. Standard deviation $= .8 \times \sigma_p = .8 \times .27 = .216$ (21.6% per year)

6. a. Portfolio standard deviation = y x .27. If client wants a standard deviation of .20, then $y = .20/.27 = 74.07\%$ in the risky portfolio.

   b. Mean return $= .07 + y \times .10 = .07 + .7407 \times .1 = .07 + .074 = .144$

7. a.

$$y^* = \frac{r_p - r_f}{A\sigma^2} = \frac{.17 - .07}{3.5 \times .27^2} = \frac{.10}{.25515} = .3919$$

So the client's optimal proportions are 39.19% in the risky portfolio and 60.81% in T-bills.

   b. Mean of optimized portfolio $= .07 + .10y^* = .07 + .3919 \times .10 = .10919$
       Standard deviation $= .3919 \times .27 = .1058$

8.

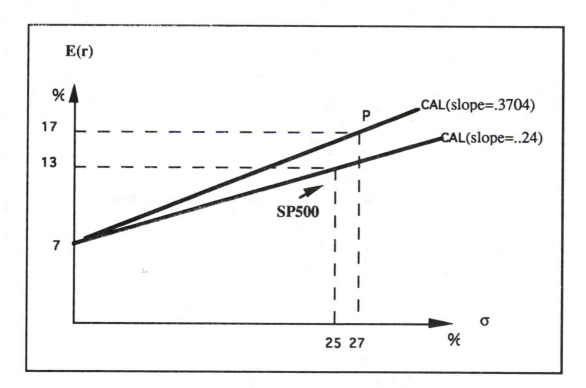

a. Slope of the CML $= \dfrac{.13 - .07}{.25} = .24$

b. My funds allow an investor to achieve a higher mean for any given standard deviation than would a passive strategy. i.e., a higher expected return for any given level of risk.

9. a. With 70% of his money in my fund's portfolio the client gets a mean of 14% per year and a standard deviation of 18.9% per year. If he shifts that money to the passive portfolio that has a mean of 13% and standard deviation of 25%, his overall mean and standard deviation would become: mean = $r_f + .7(r_M - r_f)$. Since $r_f = .07$ and $r_M = .13$,

$$\text{mean} = .07 + .7(.06) = .112.$$

The standard deviation of the complete portfolio using the passive portfolio would be:

$$\sigma_C = .7 \times .25 = .175$$

Therefore, the shift entails a decline in the mean from 14% to 11.2% and a decline in the standard deviation from 18.9% to 17.5%. Since both mean return <u>and</u> standard deviation fall, it is not yet clear whether the move is beneficial or harmful. The disadvantage of the shift is that if my client is willing to accept a mean on his total portfolio of 11.2%, he can achieve it with a lower standard deviation using my fund portfolio, rather than the passive portfolio. To achieve a target mean of 11.2%, we first write the mean of the complete portfolio as a function of the proportions invested in my fund portfolio, y:

$$r_C = .07 + y(.17 - .07) = .07 + y \times .10$$

Since our target r_C is 11.2%, the proportion that must be invested in my fund is determined as follows:

$$.112 = .07 + y \times .10, \qquad y = \frac{.112 - .07}{.10} = .42$$

The standard deviation of the portfolio would be: $\sigma_C = y \times 27 = .42 \times .27 = .1134$. So by using my portfolio, the same 11.2% mean can be achieved with a standard deviation of only 11.34% as opposed to the standard deviation of 17.5% using the passive portfolio.

b. The fee would lower the reward-to-variability ratio , i.e., the slope of the CAL. The clients would be indifferent between my fund and the passive portfolio if the slope of the CAL and the CML were equal. Let f be the fee.

$$\text{Slope of CAL with fee} = \frac{.17 - .07 - f}{.27} = \frac{.10 - f}{.27}$$

Slope of CAL without fee =.24. Setting these slopes equal we get:

$$\frac{.10 - f}{.27} = .24.$$

$$.10 - f = .27 \times .24 = .0648$$

$$f = .10 - .0648 = .0352 \text{ or } 3.52\% \text{ per year}$$

10. a. The formula for the optimal proportion to invest in the passive portfolio is:

$$y^* = \frac{r_M - r_f}{A\sigma_M^2}$$

With $r_M = .13$; $r_f = .07$; $\sigma_M = .25$; and $A = 3.5$, we get:

$$y^* = \frac{.13-.07}{3.5 \times .25^2} = .274$$

b. The answer here is the same as in 9b. The fee that you can charge a client is the same regardless of the asset allocation mix of your client's protfolio. You can charge the percent that would equalize the reward-to-variability ratio of your portfolio with that of your competition.

11. a. If 1926-1990 is assumed to be representative of future expected performance, then $A = 4$; $E(r_M) - r_f = .084$; and $\sigma_M = .211$,. So y is given by:

$$y = \frac{E(r_M) - r_f}{A\sigma_M^2} = \frac{.084}{4 \times .211^2} = .472$$

That is, 47.2% should be allocated to equity and 52.8% to bills.

b. If 1974-1990 is assumed to be representative of future expected performance, then $A = 4$; $E(r_M) - r_f = .054$; and $\sigma_M = .17$. So y is given by:

$$y = \frac{.054}{4 \times .17^2} = .467$$

Resulting in 46.7% allocated to equity and 53.3% to bills.

c. In (b) the market risk premium and the market risk are both expected to be at a lower level than in (a). This alone does not account for the changes in y. The fact that the reward-to-variability ratio is expected to be slightly lower does explain the lower proportion invested in equity.

12. Assuming no change in tastes, that is, unchanged risk aversion coefficient A, the denominator of the equation will be higher. The proportion invested in the risky portfolio will depend on the relative change in the expected risk premium (the numerator) compared to the change in the perceived market risk. Investors perceiving a higher risk will demand a higher risk premium to hold on to the same portfolio they held before. This could come about through higher expected rates of return in the equity market or lower rates in the bills market or both. However, the expectation of future rates of return are formed independently from the assessment of risk so that the expected risk premium could be higher, lower or unchanged.

13. a. $\quad\quad\quad\quad\quad\quad E(r) = 8\% = 5 + y(11 - 5)$

$$y = \frac{8 - 5}{11 - 5} = .5$$

b. $\sigma = y\sigma_p = .5 \times 15 = 7.5\%$

c. The first client is more risk averse, allowing a smaller standard deviation.

14. Assuming $r_f = 5$

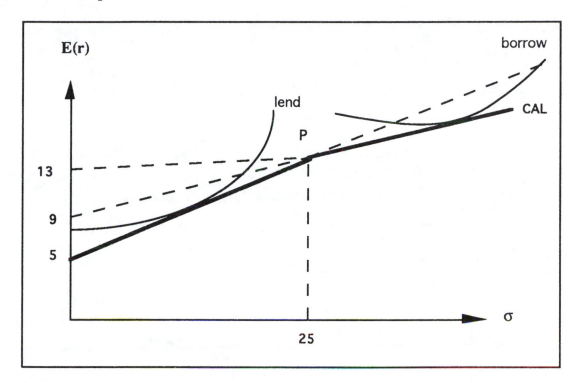

15. For lenders

$$1 \geq y = \frac{100 \; [E(r) - r_f]}{A\sigma^2}$$

$$A = \frac{100(13 - 5)}{25^2} = 1.28$$

For borrowers

$$1 \leq y = \frac{100 \; [E(r) - r_f^B]}{A\sigma^2}$$

$$A = \frac{100(13 - 9)}{625} = .64; \qquad y = 1 \text{ for } .64 \leq A \leq 1.28$$

16. a. The graph of 14 has to be redrawn here with $E(r) = 11$ and $s = 15$

b. $$A \geq \frac{100(11 - 5)}{225} = 2.67$$

$$A \leq \frac{100(11 - 9)}{225} = .89$$

$y = 1$ for $.89 \leq A \leq 2.67$

17. The fee depends on reward to variability ratio.

For lenders

$$\frac{11 - 5 - f}{15} = \frac{13 - 5}{25} \quad ; \qquad f = 6 - \frac{8 \times 15}{25} = 1.2\%$$

For borrowers

$$\frac{11 - 9 - f}{15} = \frac{13 - 9}{25} \quad ; \qquad f = 2 - \frac{15 \times 2}{25} < 0$$

The results show that the active portfolio is inferior for borrowers.

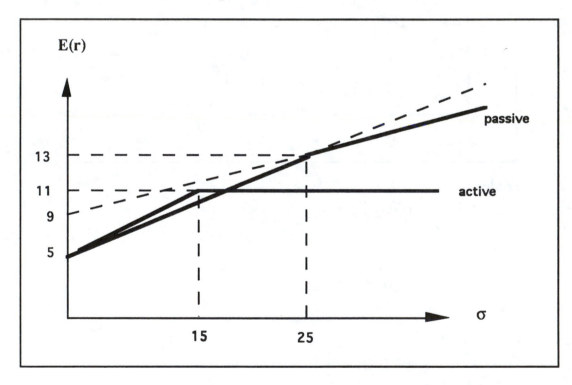

1. The parameters of the opportunity set are:

    $E(r_S) = .22$, $E(r_B) = .13$, $\sigma_S = .32$, $\sigma_B = .23$ $\rho = .15$

    From the standard deviations and the correlation coefficient we generate the covariance matrix $(Cov((r_S, r_B) = \rho\ \sigma_S\sigma_B)$:

	Bonds	Stocks
Bonds	.05290	.01104
Stocks	.01104	.10240

    The minimum variance portfolio is found by applying the formula:

    $$w_{Min}(S) = \frac{\sigma_B^2 - Cov(B,S)}{\sigma_S^2 + \sigma_B^2 - 2\ Cov(B,S)}$$

    $$= (.0529 - .01104) / (.0529 + .1024 - 2 \times .01104) = .3142$$

    $$w_{Min}(B) = .6858$$

    The minimum variance portfolio mean and standard deviation are:

    $$E(r_{Min}) = .3142 \times .22 + .6858 \times .13 = .1583$$

    $$\sigma_{Min} = [W_S^2 \times \sigma_S^2 + W_B^2 \times \sigma_B^2 + 2 \times W_S \times W_B \times Cov(S,B)]^{1/2}$$

    $$= [.3142^2 \times .1024 + .6858^2 \times .0529 + 2 \times .3142 \times .6858 \times .01104]^{1/2}$$
    $$= .19937$$

2.

% in stocks	% in bonds	Exp. return	Std dev.	
00.00	100.00	13.00	23.00	
20.00	80.00	14.80	20.37	
31.42	68.58	15.83	19.94	minimum variance
40.00	60.00	16.60	20.18	
60.00	40.00	18.40	22.50	
70.75	29.25	19.37	24.57	tangency portfolio
80.00	20.00	20.20	26.68	
100.00	00.00	22.00	32.00	

3.

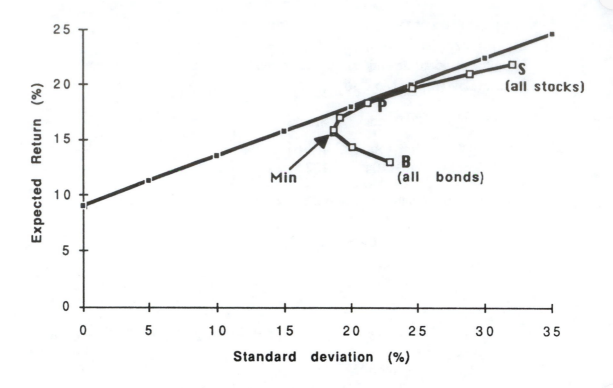

The graph shows a mean of 19.3675% and standard deviation of 24.5667%.

4. The proportions of stocks in the optimal risky portfolio is given by:

$$W_S = \frac{[E(r_S) - r_f]\sigma_S - [E(r_B) - r_f]Cov(B,S)}{[E(r_S) - r_f]\sigma_S^2 + [E(r_B) - r_f]\sigma_B^2 - [E(r_B) - r_f + E(r_B) - r_f]Cov(B,S)}$$

$$\frac{(.22 - .09).0529 - (.13 - .09).01104}{(.22 - .09).0529 - (.13 - .09).1024 - [(.22 - .09) + (.13 - .09)].01104}$$

= .7075

W_B = .2925

The mean and standard deviation of the optimal risky portfolio are:

$E(r_p)$ = .7075 x . 22 + .2925 x .13   .193675

σ_p = [.7075^2 x .1024 + .2925^2 x .0529 + 2 x .7075 x .2925 x .01104]$^{1/2}$
      = .245667

5. The reward-to-variability ratio of the optimal CAL is:

$$\frac{E(r_p) - r_f}{\sigma_p} = \frac{.193675 - .09}{.245667} = .422$$

6. a. If you require your portfolio to yield a mean return of 15% you can find the corresponding standard deviation from the optimal CAL. The formula for this CAL is:

$$E(r_C) = r_f + \frac{E(r_p) - r_f}{\sigma_p} \times \sigma_C = .09 + .422\sigma_C$$

Setting $E(r_C)$ equal to 15% we find: that the standard deviation of the optimal portfolio is 14.22%.

b. To find the proportion invested in T-bills we remember that the mean of the complete portfolio, 15%, is an average of the T-bill rate and the optimal combination of stocks and bonds, P. Let y be the proportion in this portfolio. The mean of any portfolio along the optimal CAL is:

$$E(r_C) = (1 - y)r_f + yE(r_p) = r_f + y[E(r_p) - r_f] = .09 + y(.193675 - .09).$$

Setting $E(r_C) = .15$ we find:. $15 = .09 + y(.103675)$, so $y = .5787$, and $1 - y = .4213$ is the proportion in T-bills.
To find the proportions invested in each of the stock and bond funds we multiply .5787 by the proportions of the stocks and bonds in the complete portfolio:

Proportion of stocks = .5787 x .7075 = .4094
Proportion of bonds = .5787 x .2925 = .1693

7. Using only the stock and bond funds to achieve a portfolio mean of 15% we must find the appropriate proportion y in the stock fund and $1 - y$ in the bond fund. The portfolio mean will be:

$$.15 = .22y + (1 - y).13 = .13 + .09y, \text{ and } y = .2222$$

So the proportions will be 22.22% in stocks and 77.78% in bonds. The standard deviation of this portfolio will be:

$$\sigma_p = (.2222^2 \times .1024 + .7778^2 \times .0529 + 2 \times .2222 \times .7778 \times .01104)^{1/2}$$
$$= .202175.$$

This is considerably larger than the standard deviation of .1422 achieved with T-bills and the optimal portfolio.

8. With no opportunity to borrow you wish to construct a portfolio with a mean of 29%. Since this exceeds the mean on stocks of 22%, you will have to go short on bonds, which have a mean of 13%, and use the proceeds to buy additional stock. The graphically representation of the problem is:

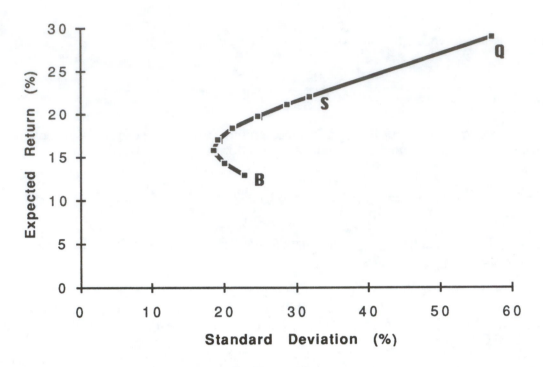

Point Q is the stock/bond combination with mean of 29%. Let y be the proportion of stocks and 1−y the proportion of bonds required to achieve the 29% mean. Then:

$$.29 = .22y + (1 - y).13 = .13 + .09y$$

$$y = 1.78, \quad \text{and } 1-y = -.78$$

Therefore, you would have to invest in stocks 1.78 times your own funds by selling short an amount of bonds equal to .78 of your own funds. The standard deviation of this portfolio would be:

$$\sigma_P = [1.78^2 \times .1024 + (-.78)^2 \times .0529 + 2(1.78)(-.78) \times .01104]^{1/2}$$
$$= .5709$$

If you were allowed to borrow at the risk-free rate of 9%, the way to achieve the target 29% would be to invest more than 100% of your funds in the optimal risky portfolio, moving out along the CAL to the right of P, up to R, on the graph below.

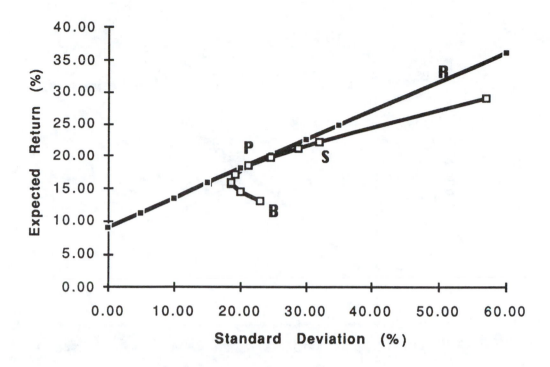

R is the point on the optimal CAL which has the mean of 29%. Using the formula for the optimal CAL we can find the corresponding standard deviation:

$$E(r) = .09 + .422\sigma$$

Setting $E(r) = .29$, we get: $.29 = .09 + .422\sigma$, so that $\sigma = .4739$, which is considerably less than the .5709 standard deviation you would get without the possibility of borrowing at the risk-free rate of .09%.
What is the portfolio composition of point R on the optimal CAL? The mean of any portfolio along this CAL is:

$$E(r) = r_f + y(r_P - r_f)$$

where y is the proportion invested in the optimal stock-bond portfolio P and r_P is the mean of that portfolio, which is 19.37.

$$.29 = .09 + y(19.37 - .09)$$
$$y = 1.93$$

This means that for every $1 of your own funds invested in portfolio P, you would borrow $.93 and invest it also in portfolio P.

9. a.

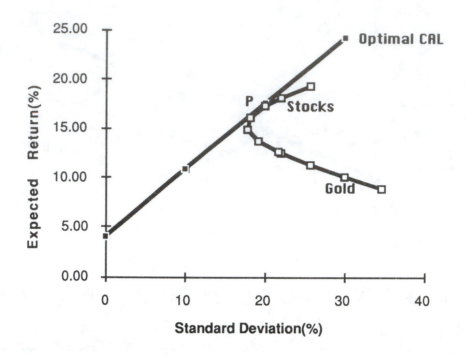

Even though gold seems dominated by stocks, it still might be an attractive asset to hold as a part of portfolio. If the correlation between gold and stocks is sufficiently low, it will be held as a portfolio diversified in the optimal tangency portfolio.

b. If gold had a correlation coefficient with stocks of +1, it would not be held. The optimal CAL would be comprised of bills and stocks only. Since the set of risk/return combinations of stocks and gold (the stock/gold CAL) plots as a straight line with a negative slope, it is all dominated by the stocks portfolio. This could not be an equilibrium. If no one were to desire gold, its price would fall and its rate of return increase until it became an attractive enough asset to hold.

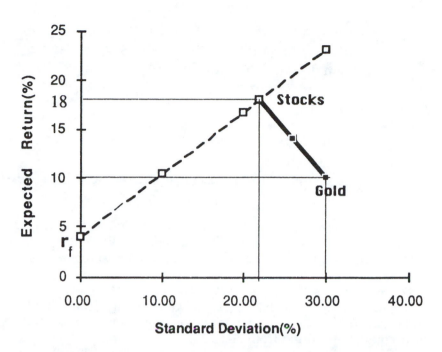

10. False. Since A and B are perfectly negatively correlated, a risk-free portfolio can be created and its rate of return in equilibrium will be the risk-free rate. To find out the proportions of this portfolio, set the standard deviation equal to zero. This reduces to the following simple relationship

$$\sigma_P = y \times .05 - (1 - y) \times .10$$

$$y = 2/3$$

The expected rate of return on this risk-free portfolio is:

$$E(r) = 2/3 \times 10\% = (1/3) \times 15\% = 11.67\%$$

Therefore, r_f must be 11.67%

11. False. if the borrowing and lending rates are not identical, then depending on the tastes of the individuals, that is the shape of their indifference curves, borrowers and lenders could have different optimal risky portfolios.

12. False. Only in the unique theoretical case where all assets are perfectly positively correlated, will the formula of the portfolio standard deviation reduce to the weighted average of all asset standard deviation. Otherwise, as the formula shows, the (smaller than +1) correlation coefficients affect the portfolio standard deviation.

13. The probability distribution is:

Probability	Rate of Return
.7	1.00 (100%)
.3	−.50 (−50%)

Mean = .7 x 1.00 + .3 x (− .5) = .55, or 55%

Mean = .7 x 1.00 + .3 x (−.5) = .55, or 55%

Variance = .7 x (1.00 − .55)^2 + .3 x (−.5 − .55)^2 = .4725

Standard deviation = .4725$^{1/2}$ = .6874

14. σ_P = .30 = yσ = 40y

y = .75

σ_{r_p} = 12 + .75(30 − 12) = 25.5%

15.a.   Restricting the portfolio to 20 stocks rather than 40-50 will increase the risk of the portfolio.

   b.   If Hennessy were to manage the restricted portfolio with the objective of minimizing risk the increase in risk would be small. But this will defeat the purpose of the exercise which is stock picking for their _mean_ which attracted the committee's attention in the first place.

16.   Risk reduction benefits from diversification are not a linear function of the number of issues in the portfolio, Rather, it is an exponentially decreasing function. Restricting Hennesey to 10 instead of 20 issues would increase the risk of his portfolio by more than restricting the portfolio from 30 to 20.

17.   The point is well taken because what the committee should be concerned with is the total risk of their entire portfolio. Since Hennessey's portfolio is only one of six well diversified portfolios and smaller than the average, the concentration in fewer issues could have a sufficiently small effect on the diversification of the total fund. So that unleashing Hennessey on stock picking may be advantageous.

18.   (d). The portfolio variance depends on the stock variances and covariance.

19.   No, as long as they are not risk neutral.

20.   No change. The same reasons apply.

CHAPTER 8 : THE CAPITAL ASSET PRICING MODEL

1. $$E(r_P) = r_f + b[E(r_M) - r_f]$$

    $$.20 = .05 + b(.15 - .05)$$

    $$b = .15/.10 = 1.5$$

2. If the covariance of the security doubles, then so will its b and its risk premium. The current risk premium is .06 = (.13 -.07), so that new risk premium would be .12, and the new discount rate for the security would be .12 + .7 = .19.
    If the stock pays a level perpetual dividend, then we know from the original data that the dividend, D, must satisfy the equation:

    Price = Dividend / Discount rate

    $$40 = D/.13$$

    $$D = 40 \times .13 = \$5.20$$

    At the new discount rate of .19, the stock would be worth only \$5.20/.19 = \$27.37. The increase in stock risk has lowered its value

3. The appropriate discount rate for the project is:

    $$r_f + b[E(r_M) - r_f] = .09 + 1.7(.19 - .09) = .26$$

    Using this discount rate,

    $$NPV = -20 + \sum_{t=1}^{10} \frac{10}{1.26^t} + \frac{10}{1.26^t}$$

    $$= -20 + 10 \times PA(26\%, 10 \text{ years}) + 10 \times PF(26\%, 10 \text{ years}) = 15.64$$

    The internal rate of return on the project is 49.55%. The highest value that b can take before the hurdle rate exceeds the IRR is determined by

    $$.4955 = .09 + b(.19 - .09)$$

    $$b = .4055/.10 = 4.055$$

4. a. False. $b = 0$ implies $E(r) = r_f$, not zero.

    b. False. Investors require a risk premium only for bearing systematic (undiversifiable or market) risk.

    c. False. 75% of your portfolio should be in the market, and 25% in bills. Then,

    $$b_P = .75 \times 1 + .25 \times 0 = .75.$$

5. a. The beta is the sensitivity of the stock's return to the market return. Call A the aggressive stock and D the defensive one. Then beta is the change in the in the stock return per change in the market return.

$$b_A = \frac{.02 - .32}{.05 - .20} = 2.0$$

$$b_D = \frac{.035 - .14}{.05 - .20} = .70$$

b. With equal likelihood of either scenarios, the expected return is an average of the two possible outcomes.

$$E(r_A) = (.02 + .32)/2 = .17$$

$$E(r_B) = (.035 + .14)/2 = .0875$$

c. The SML is determined by the market expected return of $(.20 + .05)/2 = .125$, with a β of 1, and the bill return of .08 with a b of zero.

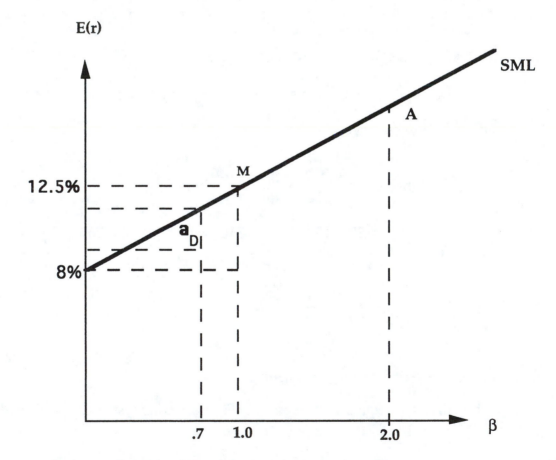

The equation of the line is:

$$E(r) = .08 + b(.125 - .08).$$

d. The aggressive stock has a fair expected return of: $E(r_A) = .08 + 2.0(.125 - .08) = .17$ and an actual expected return of .17. Thus its alpha is zero. Similarly, the fair return on the defensive stock is: $E(r_D) = .08 + .7(.125 - .08) = .1115$.

The actual expected return on D is only .0875, and

$$a_D = \text{actual expected return} = \text{required return given risk}$$
$$= .0875 - .1115 = -.024.$$

The points for each stock plot on the graph as indicated above.

e. The hurdle rate is determined by the project beta, .7. The correct discount rate is .1115 or 11.15%, the fair rate of return on stock D.

6. Not possible. Portfolio A has a higher beta than B, but its expected return is lower. Thus, A cannot exist in equilibrium.

7. Possible. If the CAPM is valid, the expected rate of return compensates only for systematic (market) risk represented by beta rather than the standard deviation which includes nonsystematic risk. Thus, A's lower rate of return can be paired with a higher standard deviation, as long as A's beta is lower than B's.

8. Not possible. The reward-to-variability ratio for portfolio A is better than that of the market, which is impossible according to CAPM, since the CAPM predicts that the market is the most efficient portfolio. Using the numbers supplied,

$$S_A = \frac{.16 - .10}{.12} = .5 \qquad S_M = \frac{.18 - .10}{.24} = .33$$

The numbers would imply that portfolio A provides a better risk-reward tradeoff than the market portfolio.

9. Not possible. Portfolio A clearly dominates the market portfolio. It has a lower standard deviation with a higher expected return.

10. Not possible. The SML for this situation is: $E(r) = .10 + b(.18 - .10)$
A portfolio with a beta of 1.5 requires an expected return of $E(r) = .10 + 1.5(.08) = .22$
A's expected return is 16%, that is, A is below the SML, and hence, is an overpriced portfolio. This is inconsistent with the CAPM.

11. Not possible. Same SML as in problem 10. Here portfolio A's required expected return is: $.10 + .9(.08) = .172$, which is still higher than .16. A is overpriced.

12. Possible. Same CML as shown in problem 8. Portfolio A plots below the CML, as any asset is expected to. This situation is not inconsistent with the CAPM.

13. Since the stock's beta is equal to 1, its expected rate of return should be equal to that of the market, that is, 18%.

$$r_1 = (P_1 + D)/P_0 - 1$$

$$.18 = (P_1 + 9)/100 - 1$$

$$P_1 = \$109$$

14. Assume that the $1,000 is a perpetuity. If beta is zero, the investment should yield the risk-free rate, 8%.

$$PV = 1000/.08 = \$12,500$$

If, however, beta is equal to 1, the investment should yield 18%, and the price paid for the firm should be:

$$PV = 1000/.18 = \$5,555.56$$

The difference, $6944.44, is what you will pay if you erroneously assumed that beta is zero rather than 1.
For a one year cash flow

$$PV\ (b=0\ ) = 1000/(1 + 08\ ) = \$\ 925.93$$

$$PV\ (b=1\ ) = 1000/(1 + .18\ ) = \$\ 847.46$$

with a difference of $78.47. For any n year cash flow the difference is:

$$1,000(P/A,8\%,n) - 1,000(P/A,18\%,n)$$

15. Using the SML: $.06 = .08 + b(.18 - .08)$

$$b = -.02/.10 = -.2$$

16. $$r_1 = .19; \quad r_2 = .16; \quad b_1 = 1.5; \quad b_2 = 1$$

a. To tell which investor was a better predictor of individual stocks we look at their alphas Alpha is the difference between their actual return and that predicted by the SML given the risk of their individual portfolios. Without information about the parameters of this equation (risk-free rate and market rate of return) we cannot tell which one is more accurate.

b. If $r_f = .06$ and $r_M = .14$, then

$$a_1 = .19 - [.06 + 1.5(.14 - .06)] = .19 - .18 = .01$$

$$a_2 = .16 - [.06 + 1(.14 - .06)] = .16 - .14 = .02$$

Here, the second investor has the larger alpha and thus he appears to be a more accurate predictor. By making better predictions the second investor appears to have tilted his portfolio toward underpriced stocks.

c. If $r_f = .03$ and $r_M = .15$, then

$$a_1 = .19 - [.03 + 1.5(.15 - .03)] = .19 - .21 = -.02$$

$$a_2 = .16 - [.03 + 1(.15 - .03)] = .16 - .15 = .01$$

Here, not only does the second investor appear to be a better predictor, but the first investor's predictions appear valueless.

17.a.   Since the market portfolio has by definition a beta of 1, its expected rate of return is 12%.

  b.   b=0 means no systematic risk,. Hence, the portfolio's fair return is the risk-free rate, 4%.

  c.   Using the SML, the fair rate of return of a stock with b= -0.5 is:

$$E(r) = .04 + (-.5)(.12 - .04) = .0\%$$

The expected rate of return, using the expected price and dividend of next year:

$$E(r) = 44/40 - 1 = .10 \text{ or } 10\%$$

This implies that the stock is underpriced.

18. a.

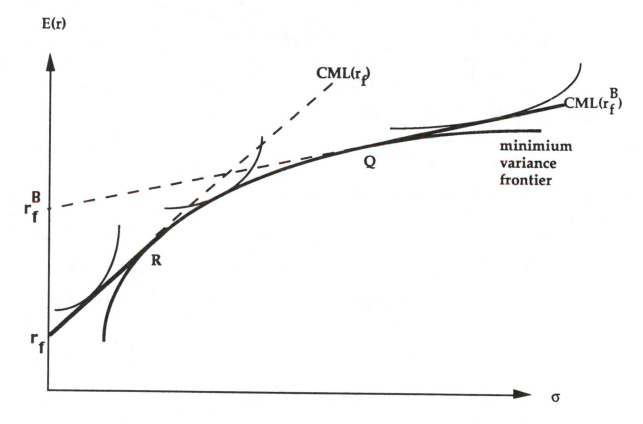

The risky portfolio selected by all defensive investors is at the tangency point between the minimum-variance frontier and the ray originating at r_f, depicted by point R on the graph. Point Q represents the risky portfolio of all aggressive investors, it is the tangency point between the minimum-variance frontier and the ray originating at r^B .

  b.   Investors who do not wish to borrow or lend will each have a unique risky portfolio at the tangency of their own individual indifference curves with the minimum-variance frontier in the section R to Q.

c. The market portfolio is clearly defined (in all circumstances) as the portfolio of all risky securities, with weights in proportion t o their market value. Thus, by design, the average investor holds the market portfolio. The average investor in turn, neither borrows nor lends. Hence, the market portfolio is on the efficient frontier between R and Q.

d. Yes, the zero-beta CAPM is valid in this scenario as shown in the graph below:

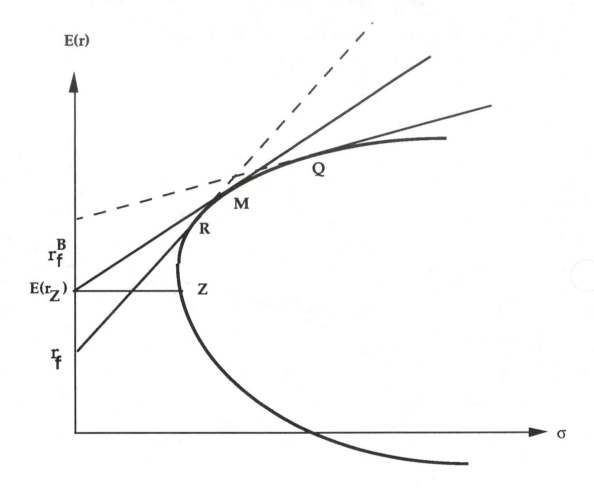

19. Assume that the stocks pay no dividend, hence, they are tax free. Then the two classes of investors draw two different CML both supported by the same efficient frontier of risky non-taxable) assets.

Note that: (l) Any combination of two efficient portfolios is efficient. (2) The average investor holds an average of T and TE, which is the market portfolio. (3) The zero-beta CAPM holds where r_f and r(t—l) are analogous to r_f and r_f^B. See graph above, problem 18(d).

20. In the zero-beta CAPM the zero-beta portfolio replaces the risk-free rate, thus,

$$E(r) = .08 + .6(.17 - .08) = .134 \quad \text{or } 13.4\%$$

CHAPTER 9: INDEX MODELS

1. a. To optimize this portfolio one would need:

$$
\begin{array}{lclll}
n & = & 75 & \text{estimates of means} \\
n & = & 75 & \text{estimates of variances} \\
\dfrac{n^2 - n}{2} & = & 2775 & \text{estimates of covariances} \\
\hline
\dfrac{n^2 + 3n}{2} & = & 2925 & \text{estimates of covariances}
\end{array}
$$

b. In a single index model: $r_i - r_f = \alpha_i + \beta_i(r_M - r_f) + e_i$

The variance of the rate of return on each stock can be decomposed into the components:

(1) $\beta_M^2 \sigma_M^2$ The variance due to the common market factor

(2) $\sigma^2(e_i)$ The variance due to firm specific unanticipated events

In this model $Cov(r_i, r_j) = \beta_i \beta_j \sigma_M^2$.

The number of parameter estimates required will be:

$n = 75$ estimates of the mean $E(r_i)$,

$n = 75$ estimates of the sensitivity coefficient β_i,

$n = 75$ estimates of the firm-specific variance $\sigma^2(e_i)$, and
1 estimate of the market mean $E(r_M)$
1 estimate for the market variance σ_M^2.

Thus, the single index model reduces the total number of required parameters estimates from 2925 to 227, and in general from $(n^2 + 3n)/2$ to $3n + 2$.

2. a. The standard deviation of each individual stock is given by:

$$
\sigma_i = [\beta_M^2 \sigma_M^2 + \sigma^2(e_i)]^{1/2}
$$

Since $\beta_A = .6$, $\beta_B = 1.3$, $\sigma(e_A) = .32$, $\sigma(e_B) = .37$ and $\sigma_M = .26$
we get:

$$
\sigma_A = (.6^2 \times .26^2 + .32^2)^{1/2} = .356
$$

$$\sigma_B = (1.3^2 \times .26^2 + .37^2)^{1/2} = .5011$$

b. The expected value of the expected rate of return on a portfolio is the weighted average of the means of the individual securities:

$$E(r_p) = w_A E(r_A) + w_B E(r_B) + w_F r_F$$

where w_A, w_B, and w_F are the portfolio weights of stock A, stock B, and T-bills, respectively.

Substituting in the formula we get:

$$E(r_p) = .33 \times .14 + .38 \times .25 + .29 \times .09 = .1673$$

The beta of the portfolio is similarly a weighted average of the betas of the individual securities:

$$\beta_P = w_A \beta_A + w_B \beta_B + w_F \beta_F$$

β_F the beta of T-bills, is zero. The beta of the portfolio is therefore:

$$\beta_P = .33 \times .6 + .38 \times 1.3 + 0 = .692$$

The total variance of this portfolio is :

$$\sigma_P^2 = \beta_P^2 \sigma_M^2 + \sigma^2(e_P)$$

where $\beta_P^2 \sigma_M^2$ is the systematic component and $\sigma^2(e_P)$ is the nonsystematic component.

Since the residuals, e_i are uncorrelated, the non-systematic variance is:

$$\sigma^2(e_P) = w_A^2 \sigma^2(e_A) + w_B^2 \sigma^2(e_B) + w_F^2 \sigma^2(e_F)$$

$$= .33^2 \times 32^2 + .38^2 \times .37^2 + 0$$

$$= .03091972$$

where $\sigma^2(e_A)$ and $\sigma^2(e_A)$ are the firm-specific or the nonsystematic variances of stocks A and B, and $\sigma^2(e_F)$ the nonsystematic variance of T-bills, which is zero. The residual standard deviation of the portfolio is thus:

$$\sigma^2(e_P) = (.03091972)^{1/2} = .1758$$

The total variance of the portfolio is then:

$$\sigma_P^2 = .692^2 \times .26^2 + .03091972 = .063291$$

and the standard deviation is .251577.

3. a. The two figures depict the stocks' characteristic lines (SCL). Stock A has a higher firm-specific risk because the deviations of the observations from the SCL are larger for A than for B. Deviations are the vertical distance of each observation from the SCL. Market beta measures systematic risk which is the slope of the SCL. B's SCL is steeper, hence B's systematic risk is greater.

RSQR of the SCL is the ratio of the explained variation of the stock's return to total variance which can be decomposed to the explained variation plus the stock's residual variance. Since B's explained variation is higher and its residual variance is smaller its RSQR is higher than A's. [The explained variation is $\beta^2 \sigma^2(M)$ which is greater the larger the beta.]

   b. Alpha is the intercept of the SCL with the expected return axis. Stock A has a small positive alpha whereas stock B has a negative alpha, that is, A's alpha is larger.

   e. The correlation coefficient is simply the square root of RSQR (see 3c.).

4. a. Firm-specific risk is measured by the residual standard deviation. Thus, stock A has more firm-specific risk, $10.3 > 9.1$.

   b. Market risk is measured by beta. A has a larger beta coefficient, $1.2 > .8$.

   c. RSQR measures the fraction of variation explained by the market return. A's RSQR is larger than B's, $.576 > .436$.

   d. The average rate of return in <u>excess</u> of that predicted by the CAPM is measured by alpha, the intercept of the SCL. Alpha(A) - .01 is larger than alpha(B) = -.02.

   e. Rewriting the SCL equation of stock A in terms of total return (r):

$$r_A - r_f = \alpha + \beta(r_M - r_f)$$
$$r_A = \alpha + r_f(1 - \beta) + \beta r_M$$

The intercept is now equal to:

$$\alpha + r_f(1 - \beta) = .01 + r_f(1 - 1.2).$$

Since $r_f = .06$,

$$\text{alpha(A)} = .01 - .012 = -.002.$$

5. The standard deviation of each stock can be derived from the following equation for RSQR:

$$\rho_i^2 = \beta_i^2 \sigma_M^2 / \sigma_i^2 = \text{Explained variation/Total variation}$$

we get

$$\sigma_A^2 = (\beta_A^2 \sigma_M^2) / \rho_A^2$$

so that,

$$\sigma_A^2 = (.65^2 \times .25^2) / .15 = .17604$$

$$s_A = .41957.$$

For stock B

$$\sigma_B^2 = (1.1^2 \times .25^2) / .30 = .25208$$

$$s_A = .50208.$$

6.   The systematic risk for A is

$$\beta_A^2 \sigma_M^2 = .65^2 \times .25^2 = .02641$$

and the firm-specific risk of A is the difference between A's total risk and its systematic risk,

$$.17604 - .02641 = .14963$$

B's systematic risk is:

$$\beta_B^2 \sigma_M^2 = 1.1^2 \times .25^2 = .076525$$

and B's firm-specific risk is:

$$.25208 - .075625 = .17646$$

7.   The covariance between the returns of A and B is:

$$\text{Cov}(r_A, r_B) = \beta_A \beta_B \sigma_M^2$$

$$= .65 \times 1.1 \times .0625 = .0446875$$

And the correlation coefficient between the returns of A and B is:

$$\rho(A,B) = \frac{Cov(r_A,r_B)}{\sigma_A \sigma_B}$$

$$= .0446875 / (.41957 \times .50208) = .21213$$

$$Cov(r_A,r_M) = \rho\sigma_A\sigma_M$$

$$= .15^{1/2} \times .41957 \times .25 = .04062$$

$$Cov(r_B,r_M) = \rho\sigma_B\sigma_M$$

$$= .30^{1/2} \times .50208 \times .25 = .06875$$

9. Non-zero alphas are inconsistent with the CAPM. The question is whether the alpha estimates reflect sampling errors of real mispricing. To test the hypothesis of whether the intercepts, of .02 for A, and .04 for B, are significantly different from zero, we must compute t-values for each intercept. To do so we need the standard deviation of the estimate of alpha.

$$t_A = \alpha_A / \sigma_A = .02 / \sigma_A(\alpha)$$

$$t_B = \alpha_B / \sigma_B = .04 / \sigma_B(\alpha)$$

The data here is not sufficient to calculate $\sigma(\alpha)$, hence, the above t-values cannot be derived. In general, a t-value of 2 or larger is significant.

10. For portfolio P we can compute:

$$\sigma_P = [.6^2 \times .17604 + .4^2 \times .25208 + 2 \times .4 \times .6 \times .0446875]^{1/2}$$

$$= [.1251572]^{1/2} = .35378$$

$$\beta_P = .6 \times .65 + .4 \times 1.1 = .83$$

$$\sigma^2(e_P) = \sigma_P^2 - \beta_B^2\sigma_P^2 = .12516 - .04305625 = .0821$$

$$Cov(r_P,r_M) = \beta_P\sigma_M^2 = .83 \times .0625 = .051875$$

This same result can be also attained using the covariances of the individual stocks with the market;

$$Cov(r_P,r_M) = Cov(.6r_P + .4r_B, r_M)$$

$$= .6\text{Cov}(r_P, r_M) + .4\text{Cov}(r_B, r_M)$$

$$= .6 \times .04062 + .4 \times .06875 = .051872$$

11. For portfolio Q:

$$\sigma_Q = [.5^2 \times .17604 + .3^2 \times .25208 + 2 \times .5 \times .3 \times .0446875]^{1/2}$$

$$= [.08010]^{1/2} = .2830255$$

$$\beta_Q = .5 \times .65 + .3 \times 1.1 = .655$$

$$\sigma^2(e_Q) = \sigma_Q^2 - \beta_Q^2 \sigma_P^2 = .08010 - .026814 = .053286$$

$$\text{Cov}(r_Q, r_M) = \beta_Q \sigma_M^2 = .655 \times .0625 = .0409375$$

12. In a two stock capital market, the capitalization of A being twice that of B, means that

$$w_A = 2/3 \text{ and } w_B = 1/3. \quad \sigma_A = .3, \ \sigma_B = .5, \ \rho(A,B) = .7$$

a. The standard deviation of the market index portfolio is:

$$\sigma_M^2 = w_A^2 \sigma_A^2 + w_B^2 \sigma_B^2 + 2w_A w_B \rho \ \sigma_A \sigma_B$$

$$= (2/3)^2 (.30)^2 + (1/3)^2 (.50)^2 + 2 \ (2/3) \ (1/3) \ (.7)(\ .30) \ (.50)$$

$$= .11444$$

$$\sigma_M = [.11444]^{1/2} = .3383$$

b. The beta of each stock is:

$$\beta_A = \text{Cov}(r_A, r_M) / \sigma_M^2$$

where

$$\text{Cov}(r_A, r_M) = \text{Cov}[r_A, (.6666 r_A + .3333 r_B)]$$

$$= .6666 \sigma_A^2 + .3333 \text{Cov}(r_A, r_B)$$

$$= (2/3) \ .30^2 + (1/3)(.7)(.3)(.5)$$

$$= .095$$

so that,

$$\beta_A = \frac{.095}{.11444} = .83$$

For stock B

$$\text{Cov}(r_B, r_M) = \text{Cov}[\, r_B, \,(.6666r_A + .3333r_B)\,]$$

$$= .6666\text{Cov}(r_A, r_B) + .3333\sigma_B^2$$

$$= (2/3)(.7)(.3)(.5) + (1/3).5^2 = .15333$$

so that,

$$\beta_B = \frac{.15333}{.11444} = 1.34$$

c. The residual variance of each stock is:

$$\sigma^2(e_A) = \sigma_A^2 - \beta_A^2\sigma_M^2$$

$$= .3^2 - .83^2 \times .11444$$

$$= .011162284$$

$$\sigma(e_A) = .10565$$

$$\sigma^2(e_B) = \sigma_B^2 - \beta_B^2\sigma_M^2$$

$$= .5^2 - 1.34^2 \times .11444$$

$$= .044512$$

$$\sigma(e_B) = .21098$$

d. If the index model holds, then the following holds too,

$$(r_A - r_f) = \beta_A(r_M - r_f)$$

$$.11 = .83\,(r_M - r_f)$$

Thus the market risk premium must be

$$(r_M - r_f) = .11/.83 = .1325$$

Since A's beta is smaller than 1.0, its risk premium is smaller than the market's risk premium .

13. a. Merrill Lynch adjusts beta by taking the sample estimate of beta and averaging it with 1.0, using the weights of 2/3 and 1/3, as follows:

$$\text{adjusted beta} = (2/3)1.24 + (1/3)1 = 1.16$$

   b. If you use your current estimate of beta to be $\beta_{t-1} = 1.24$, then

$$\beta_t = .3 + .7(1.24) = 1.168$$

   which is the prediction of beta for next year.

14.   [From CFA study Guide - verbatim]
   The regression results provide quantitative measures of return and risk based on annualized quarterly returns over the 1971-1980 period.

   KM: β for KM is .69, considerably below the average stock's β of 1.0, indicating when the S&P 500 Stock Index rises or falls one percentage point, KM's return on averages rises or falls 0.69 percentage point. As such it indicates KM's systematic risk or market risk is quite low relative to the market for stocks. KM's α or unique return was -3.68%, indicating that when the market return was zero percent, KM declined almost 4%, on average. KM's unsystematic or residual risk, as measured by $\sigma(e)$, was 13.02%. Its ρ was +.49, indicating a fairly close fit of the KM/S&P 500 return points to the linear regression, given that the relationship was statistically significant at the .001 level.

   WMT: β for WMT was somewhat higher at .97, indicating WMT's return pattern was very similar to the market index's β of unity and the stock therefore had average systematic risk over the period examined. α for WMT was positive and quite large, indicating an almost 14% return, on average, for WMT independent of market return. Residual risk was 21.45%, half again as much as KM, indicating a wider scatter of observations around the regression line for WMT. Correspondingly the fit of the regression model was less at a ρ of +.43 and statistical significance at the .0051 level, indicating less of WMT's returns were explained by returns on the market than was true for KM.

   The effect of including one stock or the other in a diversified portfolio may be quite different, if it can be assumed that both stocks' betas will remain stable over time, since there is such a large difference in their systematic risk level. The betas obtained from Brokerage Houses A and B may help the analyst draw inferences for the future. KM's β estimates are similar regardless of the differencing interval and time period of the underlying data. They range from .69 to 80, all well below the market average β of 1.0. WMT's β varies significantly among the three sources of calculations, ranging as high as 1.45 for the weekly price change observations over the most recent year. One could infer that WMT's for the future might be well above 1.0, meaning it may have some what more systematic risk than was implied by the quarterly regression for the 1971-1980 period.

   The upshot is that these stocks appear to have significantly different systematic risk characteristics. If equal dollar amounts are assumed invested in each, KM should reduce portfolio return volatility whereas WMT is likely to add to it.

Authors' Comment

Note that A's estimates are based on daily rates of the most recent year, while B's estimates are based on monthly rates of the 5 most recent years, and "the analyst's" estimates are based on quarterly data stretching over 10 years. Thus, sampling differences would affect results. Actually, the data suggest a trend in the estimates of beta going from the shortest sample to the longest.

1yr	5 yrs	10 yrs	
.80	.75	.69	for KM
1.45	1.20	.97	for WMT

It appears that the betas of the two stocks were changing over the last 10 years. Since we are interested in the future risk-return relationship estimates from more recent data may be more appropriate.

15. a. The α of stock A is:

$$\alpha_A = r_A - r_f - \beta_A(r_M - r_f)$$

$$= 11 - 6 - .8(12 - 8) = .2\%$$

$$\alpha_B = 14 - 6 - 1.5(12 - 8) = -.1\%$$

Stock A would be a good addition. A short position in B may be desirable.

b. The reward to variability ratio of the stocks is :

$$S_A = \frac{11 - 6}{10} = .5$$

$$S_B = \frac{14 - 6}{11} = .73$$

Stock B is superior where only one can be held.

1.   A revised estimate of the expected rate of return of the stock, would be the old estimate plus the sum of the expected change in the factors times the sensitivity coefficients, that is:

$$\text{revised } r_i = .14 + 1(.01) + .4(.01) = .154$$

2.   Equation 10.5 applies here.

$$E(r_p) = r_f + \beta_{p1}[E(r_1) - r_f] + \beta_{p2}[E(r_2) - r_f]$$

We need to find the risk premium of these two factors; $[E(r_1) - r_f]$ and $[E(r_2) - r_f]$. To do so, the following two equations with two unknowns must be solved:

$$.40 = .07 + 1.8\gamma_1 + 2.1\gamma_2$$

$$.10 = .07 + 2.0\gamma_1 + (-.5)\gamma_2$$

$$\gamma_1 = .0447 \quad \text{and} \quad \gamma_2 = .1188$$

Thus, the expected return-beta relationship is:

$$E(r_p) = .07 + .0447\beta_{p1} + .1188\beta_{p2}$$

3.   The expected return of portfolio F equals the risk-free rate since its beta equals 0. Portfolio A's ratio of risk premium to beta is: $(.10 - .04)/1 = .06$, whereas, portfolio E's ratio is higher at $(.09 - .04)/(2/3) = .075$. This implies that an arbitrage opportunity exist. For instance, you can create a portfolio G with beta equal to 1 (same as A's) by taking a long position in E and a short position in F, that is, borrowing at the risk-free rate and investing the proceeds in portfolio E. For beta of G to equal 1, the proportion, w, of funds invested in E must be $3/2 = 1.5$. The expected return of G is then;

$$E(r_G) = (-.50)(.04) + (1.5)(.09) = .115$$

$$\beta_G = (1.5)(2/3) = 1$$

Comparing G to A; G has the same beta and higher return. Now, consider portfolio H which includes a short position in A, investing the proceeds in G,

$$\beta_H = 1\beta_A + (-1)\beta_G = 1 \times 1 + (-1)1 = 0$$
$$E(r_H) = 1r_A + (-1)r_G = 1 \times .10 + (-1).115 = .015$$

The result is a zero investment portfolio (all proceeds of the short sale of A are invested in G) with a zero risk ($\beta = 0$) and the portfolios are well diversified) and a positive return of

1.5%. H is an arbitrage portfolio.

4. a. As a first step convert the scenario rates of return to dollar payoffs per share, as shown in the table below:

	Price	Scenarios 1	2	3
A	$10	10(1 − .15) = $ 8.5	10(1 + .20) = $12	10(1 + .30) = $13
B	$15	15(1 + .25) = $18.75	15(1 + .10) = $16.5	15(1 − .10) = $13.5
C	$50	50(1 + .12) = $56	50(1 + .15) = $57.5	50(1 + .12) = $56

Identifying an arbitrage opportunity always involves a zero investment portfolio. This portfolio must show non negative payoffs in all scenarios.

For example; the proceeds from selling short two shares of A and two shares of B will be sufficient to buy one share of C.

$$(-2)10 + (-2)15 + 50 = 0$$

The payoff table for this zero investment portfolio for all scenarios is:

	Price	# of shares	Investment	Scenarios 1	2	3
A	$10	−2	−20	−17	−24	−26
B	$15	−2	−30	−37.5	−33	−27
C	$50	+1	50	56	57.5	56
			$0	+1.5	+.5	+3

This portfolio qualifies as an arbitrage portfolio because it is both a zero investment portfolio and has positive returns in all scenarios.

b. Should prices of A and B go down due to excess short selling and price of C go up because of buying pressures, then the rate of return on (A + B) will go up and C's will go down.

A program that checks for the elimination of all arbitrage opportunities will constrain the portfolio proportion so that total invested equals zero. It will then require that the best scenario for any such portfolio will have positive payoff while the worst scenario for any such portfolio will have a negative payoff.

We now show a price change that is guaranteed to eliminate the arbitrage opportunity shown in 19a. First note that as the price of C changes, so will the proportion of any zero investment portfolio. Second, the weakest scenario for a portfolio long on C and short on (A + B) appears to be scenario 2. Holding equal the number of shares of A and B sold short, we solve for zero payoff in scenario 2. Denote by X the number of shares of A and B sold short and let the proceeds be sufficient to long one share of C. Now we set the the payoff in scenario 2 to zero:

$$12X + 16.5X + 57.5 = 0 \quad ; \quad X = -2.0175$$

meaning that we short 2.0175 shares of A and shares of B for each share of C held long. (Note that in the previous arbitrage portfolio X = -2).

Next, with these shares of A and B short, we ask: what is the price of one share of C that would get the portfolio investment to zero?

$$10X + 15X + P_C = 0$$

where P_C is the new price of C. Substituting X=-2.0175 we get:

$$10(-2.0175) + 15(-2.0175) + P_C = 0$$

$$P_C = 50.4375$$

This means that the minimum price change that is needed to eliminate the arbitrage opportunity is greater than 43.75 cents. To check our result, lets look at the following payoff table for a price change of 50 cents, that is, $P_C = \$50.50$.

	Price	# of shares	Investment	Scenarios 1	2	3
A	$10	−2.02	−20.2	−17.17	−24.24	−26.26
B	$15	−2.02	−30.3	−37.875	−33.33	−27.27
C	$50.50	+1	50.50	56	57.5	56
			$0	+.955	-.07	+2.47

Note that the zero investment portfolio must be recalculated (X = -2.02) and indeed the payoffs are no longer positive across the board but negative for scenario 2. Thus the arbitrage opportunity has been eliminated. This exercise proves that the price increase of C will eliminate the arbitrage opportunity we found in 4a, the one that uses an equal number of shares of A and B to go short. However, it does not eliminate all arbitrage opportunities. For example, with $P_C = \$50.50$ an arbitrage portfolio can be formed with X_A=-1.95, and X_B=-2.07 for the number of shares held short of A and B respectively.

5. Substituting the portfolio return and the betas in the expected return-beta relationship, we obtain two equations in the unknowns, the risk-free rate and the factor risk premium, F.

$$.14 = r_f + 1(F - r_f)$$

$$.148 = r_f + 1.1(F - r_f)$$

From the first equation F = .14. Substituting into the second equation, we get:

$$.148 = r_f + 1.1(.14 - r_f)$$

$$r_f = (.148 - .154)/(1. - 1.1) = (-.006)/(-.1) = .06$$

The risk-free rate is 6%

6. a. Shorting equally the 10 negative alpha stocks using the proceeds equally in the 10 positive alpha stocks eliminates the market effect and creates a zero investment portfolio. The expected dollar return is:

$$1,000,000 \times .03 + (-1,000,000)(-.03) = \$60,000.$$

Beta of this portfolio is zero because it is equally weighted, half of the weights are negative and all betas equal to one. Thus, the systematic component of the total risk is also zero. The variance of the analyst's profit is not zero, however, since this portfolio is not well diversified. Total variance amounts to the non-systematic risk.

$$\sigma^2 = \sigma^2(e_p) = (1/n)\sigma^2(e_i)$$

$$= (1/20)(.30)^2$$

$$= .0045 \quad and \quad \sigma = .06708$$

b. The only change from increasing the number of stocks is that the portfolio variance falls to:

$$\sigma^2(50) = (1/50)(.30)^2 = .0018 \quad and \quad \sigma = .04243$$

$$\sigma^2(100) = (1/100)(.30)^2 = .0009 \quad and \quad \sigma = .03$$

7 a.

$$\sigma^2 = \beta^2 \sigma_M^2 + \sigma^2(e)$$

$$\sigma_A^2 = .8^2 \times .04 + .05 = .0756$$

$$\sigma_B^2 = 1.0^2 \times .04 + .01 = .05$$

$$\sigma_C^2 = 1.2^2 \times .04 + .10 = .1576$$

b. If there are infinite number of assets with identical characteristics, a well diversified portfolio of each type will only have the systematic risk since the non-systematic risk will approach zero with large n. The mean will equal that of the individual (identical) stocks.

c. No, there is no arbitrage opportunity because the well diversified portfolios ae all on the security market line (SML).

8. a. An equally weighted portfolio P of stocks A and B will have $\beta_P = \beta_C$. Hence, a long position in C will make an arbitrage portfolio with zero investment, zero beta and positive rate of return.

b. The argument in a. leads to the proposition that the coefficient of β^2 must be zero

9.   The Factors in an APT equation have to be independent well diversified portfolios. The number of well diversified uncorrelated portfolios in the economy is limited. Parsimony and tractability of these portfolios are also important.

10.   The APT factors must correlate with major sources of uncertainty. Researchers should investigate factors that correlate with expected changes in consumption and investment opportunities. GNP, inflation rate, interest rates, are factors that can be expected to determine risk premium. In particular, industrial production (IP) is a good indicator of expected changes in the business cycle. Thus, IP is a candidate for a factor that is highly correlated with uncertainties that have to do with investment opportunities in the economy.

11. a. $E(r) = 6 + 1.2 \times 6 + .5 \times 8 + .3 \times 3 = 18.1\%$

    b. The surprise in the macro economic factors will result in a surprise rate of change in the price of the stock:

    $$\frac{\Delta P}{P} = 1.2\,(4 - 5) + (6 - 3) + .3\,(0 - 2) = 3.5\%$$

12.   The APT required return on the stock is:

    $$E(r) = 6 + 1 \times 6 + .5 \times 2 + .75 \times 4 = 16\%$$

    The suggested formula calls for $E(r) = 15\%$, hence the stock is overpriced.

CHAPTER 11: EMPIRICAL EVIDENCE ON SECURITY RETURNS

A General Note

In the following solutions to the end-of-chapter-problems, the focus is on the estimation procedure. To make it easy the number of observation was limited to four years and six portfolios. The idea is to make calculations easy enough so that students can perform them manually with the aid of a calculator. The data was generated to conform to CAPM assumptions, so that return expectations and actual rates of return equal expectations plus random noise. However, due to the very small sample, the estimates do not manifest the properties that are found in larger samples. The consequence is that the results of this small experiment are not always consistent with the findings of other studies that are reported in the chapter itself.

We have chosen to use Lotus 1-2-3 to run the regressions and the output is provided below. In Lotus, y stands for the dependent variable, x for the independent variable and e for the residual. The slope coefficient is denoted by "x coefficient(s)" and the intercept by "constant". For the summary tables some additional computations are needed. Formulas used are:

(1) Residual variance adjusted for degrees of freedom

$$\sigma_e^2 = \sigma^2(e)_{[df]} - \sigma^2(y) [1 - R^2] [n/(n-k)]$$

where n is the number of observations and k is the number of independent variables plus one (to account for the intercept).

(2) Standard deviation of beta

$$\sigma(\beta) = [\sigma_e^2 / \Sigma(x_i - \bar{x})^2]^{1/2} - [\sigma_e^2 / (n\sigma_x^2)]^{1/2}$$

(3) Standard deviation of alpha

$$\sigma(\alpha) = [\sigma_e^2 / \Sigma x_i^2]$$

(4) t-value of beta coefficient

$$t(\beta) = \beta / \sigma(\beta)$$

(5) t-value of alpha coefficient

$$t(\alpha) = \alpha / \sigma(\alpha)$$

1. **First-pass regression**

Year	Market Index	A	B	C	D	E	F
1	26.40	38.10	32.60	23.60	15.20	11.90	38.00
2	17.90	21.90	20.20	17.60	14.60	11.80	19.80
3	13.40	13.40	15.10	13.00	13.20	9.00	14.40
4	10.60	9.80	10.40	11.40	12.10	11.00	9.70
Mean	17.0750	20.8000	19.5750	16.4000	13.7750	10.9250	20.4750
Std	5.9805	10.9117	8.2802	4.7392	1.2091	1.1648	10.7307
β		1.8219	1.3828	0.7898	0.1882	0.1146	1.7821
α		-10.3084	-4 0356	2 9135	10.5612	8.9674	-9.9540
R^2		0.9971	0.9974	0.9935	0.8667	0.3465	0.9865
$\sigma^2(e)$ [df=2]		0.6951	0.3501	0.2942	0.3897	1.7735	3.1166
$Std(\beta)$		0.0697	0.0495	0.0453	0.0522	0.1113	0.1476
$Std(\alpha)$		I.7835	1.2657	1.1603	1.3353	2.8487	3.7764
$t(\beta)$		26.1366	27.9513	17.4172	3.6064	1.5297	12.0741
$t(\alpha)$		-5.7799	-3.1883	2.5111	7.9093	3.1479	-2.6359

Regression Output:A

Constant	-10.3083
Std Err of Y Est.	0.833753
R Square	0.997080
No. of observations	4
Degrees of Freedom	2
X Coefficient(s)	1.821867
Std Err of Coef.	0.069705

Regression Output:B

Constant	-4.03556
Std Err of Y Est.	0.591717
R Square	0.997446
No. of observations	4
Degrees of Freedom	2
X Coefficient(s)	1.382756
Std Err of Coef.	0.049470

Regression Output:C

Constant	2.913533
Std Err of Y Est.	0.542412
R Square	0.993450
No. of observations	4
Degrees of Freedom	2
X Coefficient(s)	0.789830
Std Err of Coef.	0.045348

Regression Output:D

Constant	10.56122
Std Err of Y Est.	0.624231
R Square	0.866724
No. of observations	4
Degrees of Freedom	2
X Coefficient(s)	0.188215
Std Err of Coef	0.052188

Regression Output:E

Constant	8.967373
Std Err of Y Est.	1.331723
R Square	0.346480
No. of observations	4
Degrees of Freedom	2
X Coefficient(s)	0.114648
Std Err of Coef.	0.111338

Regression Output:F

Constant	-9.95398
Std Err of Y Est.	1.765396
R Square	0.986466
No. of observations	4
Degrees of Freedom	2
X Coefficient(s)	1.782078
Std Err of Coef.	0.147595

2. The second-pass regressions test the hypotheses that the intercept of the regression equals zero and that the slope equals the mean excess market return, here, 17.075%.

3. **Second-pass regressions**

Portfolio	Yr 1	Yr 2	Yr 3	Yr 4	Average (y)	β from first-pass (x)
A	38.1	21.9	13.4	9.8	20.800	1.821867
B	32.6	20.2	15.1	10.4	19.575	1.382756
C	23.6	17.6	13.0	11.4	16.400	0.789836
D	15.2	14.6	13.2	12.1	13.775	0.188215
E	11.9	11.8	9.0	11.0	10.925	0.114648
F	38.0	19.8	14.4	9.7	20.475	1.782078
Mean	26.5667	17.6500	13.0167	10.7333	16.9917	1.0132
Std	10.4343	3.4813	1.9394	0.8596	3.6700	0.6976

Regression results (average on beta from first-pass):

β	5.1205
α	11.8034
R^2	0.9473
Std(β)	0.6041
Std(α)	21.1183
t(β)	8.4760
t(α)	0.5589

4. In the first-pass regressions the betas range from .1882 to 1.8219, whereas the alphas range, roughly, from +10 to -10. The pattern is as expected, the portfolios with beta larger than 1 have negative alphas and the portfolios with betas smaller than 1 have positive alphas.

    In the second-pass regression, alpha = 11.8034 and is not significantly different from zero since its t-value is smaller than 2. The slope of the SML, 5.1205, is significantly different from zero, and also significantly different from the expected mean excess market rate of return 17.075. The line is, again, too flat.

5. Due to grouping, the first-pass regression sample shrinks significantly to 3 portfolios so that the second-pass regression is based on 3 observations only. With this in mind, the intercept of the second-pass regression is 11.853, almost identical to the one found without grouping. The slope, 5.0714, is even flatter than before. Thus, no benefits from grouping can be seen. (The grouping procedure works in expectation, and did not work in the sample here).

First-pass regression (before grouping)

Year	Market Index	A	B	C	D	E	F
1	26.40	38.10	32.60	23.60	15.20	11.90	38.00
2	17.90	21.90	20.20	17.60	14.60	11.80	19.80
3	13.40	13.40	15.10	13.00	13.20	9.00	14.40
4	10.60	9.80	10.40	11.40	12.10	11.00	9.70
β		1.8219	1.3828	0.7898	0.1882	0.1146	1.7821
Rank		(1)	(3)	(4)	(5)	(6)	(2)

Grouping by betas and first-pass regressions

Year	Market Index	A+F	B+C	D+E
1	26.40	38.05	28.10	13.55
2	17.90	20.85	18.90	13.20
3	13.40	13.90	14.05	11.10
4	10.60	9.75	10.90	11.55
Mean	17.0750	20.6375	17.9875	12.3500
Std	5.9805	10.8071	6.4968	1.0446
β		1.8020	1.0863	0.1514
α		-10.1312	-0.5610	9.7643
R^2		0.9944	1.0000	0.7516
$\sigma^2(e)$ [df=2]		1.3083	0.0032	0.5421
Std(β)		0.0956	0.0047	0.0616
Std(α)		2.4467	0.1213	1.5750
t(β)		18.8439	229.0719	2.4600
t(α)		-4.14076	-4.62376	6.199602

Second-pass regression (grouping)

Year	1	2	3	4	Average (y)	β (x)
A+F	38.05	20.85	13.90	9.75	20.6375	1.801972
B+C	28.10	18.90	14.05	10.90	17.9875	1.086296
D+E	13.55	13.20	11.10	11.55	12.35	0.151432
Mean	26.5667	17.6500	13.0167	10.7333	16.9917	1.0132
Std	10.0607	3.2458	1.3567	0.7442	3.4559	0.6758

Regression results (average on beta from first-pass):

β	5.0714
α	11.8532
R^2	0.9835
$\sigma^2(e)$ [df=1]	0.5900
Std(β)	0.6562
Std(α)	1.3842
t(β)	7.7286
t(α)	8.5630

6.   Roll's critique is applicable here .o the extent that. the index is not the true market portfolio.

7.   The mean and variance of the six portfolios and the market portfolio are:

	Mean excess return((%)	Standard deviation(%)
Market	17.075	5.98
A	20.800	10.92
B	19.775	8.28
C	16.400	4 74
D	13.755	1.21
E	10.925	1.16
F	20.475	10.73

These portfolios can be plotted in the mean-standard deviation space, as shown below. The CML is the line that goes through M, the market portfolio, and the (0,0) point. (Not r_f, since these are excess rates of return). If CAPM holds, the portfolios should form an efficient frontier that is tangent to the CML at the market portfolio, M. In this examples portfolios C,D, and E appear to be inefficient, because they are underpriced and lie above the CML. This result, however, is not statistically significant due to the small sample.

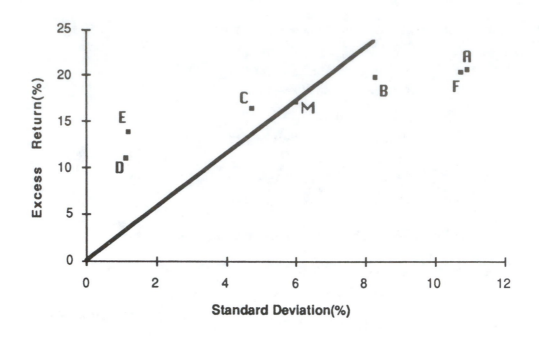

8. **Two Factors - First Pass Regrssion**

	Market Index	F2	A	B	C	D	E	F
	26.40	13.00	38.10	32.60	23.60	15.20	11.90	38.00
	17.90	17.00	21.90	20.20	17.60	14.60	11.80	19.80
	13.40	-21.00	13.40	15.10	13.00	13.20	9.00	14.40
	10.60	27.00	9.80	10.40	11.40	12.10	11.00	9.70
Mean	17.0750	9.0000	20.8000	19.5750	16.4000	13.7750	10.9250	20.4750
Std	5.9805	18.0555	10.9117	8.2802	4.7392	1.2091	1.1648	10.7307
β_1			1.81506	1.38799	0.78563	0.18977	0.10130	1.78492
β_2			0.02588	-0.0199	0.01599	-0.0059	0.05075	-0.0108
α			-10.425	-3.9456	2.84134	10.5879	8.73832	-9.9051
R^2			0.99890	0.99932	0.99713	0.87451	0.96082	0.98679
$\sigma^2(e)$ [df=1]			0.52320	0.18623	0.25724	0.73379	0.21260	6.08166
Std(β_1)			0.06047	0.03607	0.04240	0.07161	0.03854	0.20617
Std(β_2)			0.02003	0.01195	0.01404	0.02372	0.01276	0.06829
Std(α)								
t(β_1)			30.0140	38.4704	18.5273	2.64985	2.62803	8.65722
t(β_2)			1.29223	-1.6676	1.13894	-0.2500	3.97534	-0.1584

9. The second-pass regression hypotheses in a two-factor model (using excess returns) are:

    (i) The intercept of the cross-sectional regression is equal to zero.

    (ii) The first cross-sectional regression coefficient is equal to the mean excess return of the first factor, here the mean of the excess return on the market index   17.075.

    (iii) The second cross-sectional regression coefficient is equal to the mean excess return of the second factor, here 9.0.

10. The regression coefficients of the first factor (market index) range from .10130 to 1.8977. For the second factor the coefficients range from -.0199 to .05075. To answer the question look at the t-values of the regression coefficients of the first-pass regressions. This sample's results do not suggest a strong two-factor economy since the t-values of the second factor are low for five out of the six portfolios, that is, not significant.

11. A candidate for any factor portfolio should maximize the correlation with he factor itself.

12. [From the CFA Study Guide - 1984 pages 254-255]

a. The basic procedure in portfolio evaluation is to compare the returns on a managed portfolio to the return expected on an unmanaged portfolio having the same risk, via use of the CAPM. That is, expected return is calculate from:

$$E(r_p) = r_f + b_P[E(r_M) - r_f]$$

Where rf is the risk-free rate, $E(r_M)$ is the unmanaged portfolio (or the market) return and b_P is the beta coefficient (or systematic risk) of the managed portfolio. The benchmark of performance then is the unmanged portfolio. The typical proxy for this unmanged portfolio is some aggregate stock market index such as the S&P 400.

b. The benchmark error often occurs because the unmanaged portfolio used in the evaluation process is not "optimized ". That is, market indices, such as the S&P500, chosen as benchmarks are not on the evaluator's ex ante mean/variance efficient frontier. Benchmark error may also occur because of an error in the estimation of the risk-free return. Together, these two sources of error will cause the implied Security Market Line (SML) to be mispositioned.

c. The main ingredients are that the true risk-free rate is lower than the measured risk-free rate and the true market return is above the measured market return. he result is under performance relative to the true SML rather than superior performance relative to the measured SML.

CHAPTER 12: MARKET EFFICIENCY

1. Zero. If not, one could use returns from one period to predict returns in later periods and make abnormal profits.

2. c. This is a predictable pattern in returns which should not occur if the weak-form EMH is valid.

3. c. This is a classic filter rule which should not work in an efficient market.

4. b. This is the definition of an efficient market.

5. c. The P/E ratio is public information and should not predict abnormal security returns.

6. No. Wal-mart's continuing high return on assets does not imply that stock market investors who purchased Wal-mart shares after its success already was evident would have earned a high return on their investments.

7. The question for market efficiency is whether investors can earn abnormal risk-adjusted profits. If the stock price run-up occurs when only insiders are aware of the coming dividend increase, then it is a violation of strong-form, but not semi-strong form efficiency. If the public already knows of the increase, then it is a violation of semi-strong form efficiency.

8. While positive beta stocks will respond well to favorable new information about the economy's progress through the business cycle, they should not show abnormal returns around already anticipated events. If a recovery, for example, already is anticipated, the actual recovery is not news. The stock price already should reflect the coming recovery.

9. a. Consistent. Half of managers should beat the market based on pure luck in any year.

   b. Inconsistent. This would be the basis of an "easy money" rule: simply invest with last year's best managers.

   c. Consistent. Predictable *volatility* does not convey a means to earn abnormal returns.

   d. Inconsistent. The abnormal performance ought to occur in January when earnings are announced.

   e. Inconsistent. Reversals offer a means to earn easy money: just buy last week's losers.

10. Expected rates of return will differ because of differential risk premiums.

11. The excess return on the market was $8\% - 1\% = 7\%$. Therefore, the forecast excess return on GM given the market's return is $.10\% + 1.1 \times 7\% = 7.8\%$.

    GM's actual excess return was 6%, meaning that the abnormal return was -1.8%.

12. a. Based on broad market trends, AmbChaser stock should have increased by $1\% + 2.0(1.5\% - 1\%) = 2\%$. Its firm-specific (nonsystematic) return due to the lawsuit is $1 million per $100 million initial equity, or 1%. The total return should be 3%. (It is assumed here that the outcome of the lawsuit had a zero expected value).

    b. If the settlement was expected to be $2 million, then the actual settlement was a "$1 million disappointment," and so the firm-specific return would be -1%, for a total return of $2\% - 1\% = 1\%$.

13. Given market performance, predicted returns on the two stocks would be:

    Apex: $.2\% + 1.4 \times 3\% = 4.4\%$

    Bpex: $-.1\% + .6 \times 3\% = 1.7\%$

    Apex underperformed this prediction; Bpex overperformed. We conclude that Bpex won the suit.

14. Implicit in the dollar-cost averaging strategy is the notion that stock prices fluctuate around a "normal" level. Otherwise, there is no meaning to statements like, "when the price is high." How do we know, for example, that a price of $25 today will turn out to be viewed as high or low compared to the stock price in 6 months?

15. No. The value of dividend predictability already will be reflected in the stock price.

16. The market responds positively to *new* news. If the eventual recovery is anticipated, then the recovery already is reflected in stock prices. Only a better-than-expected recovery should affect stock prices.

17. Over the long haul, there is an expected upward drift in stock prices based on their fair expected rates of return. The fair expected return over any single day is very small (e.g., 12% per year is only about .03% per day), so that on any day the price is virtually equally likely to

rise or fall. However, over longer periods, the small expected daily returns cumulate, and upward moves are indeed more likely than downward ones.

18. Buy. The firm is in your view not as bad as everyone else believes it to be. Therefore, you view the firm as undervalued by the market. You are less pessimistic about the firm's prospects than the beliefs built into the stock price.

19. The negative abnormal returns (downward drift in CAR) just prior to stock purchases suggest that insiders deferred their purchases until *after* bad news was released to the public. This is evidence of valuable inside information. The positive abnormal returns after purchase suggest insider purchases in anticipation of good news. The analysis is symmetric for insider sales.

20. Here we need a two-factor model relating Ford's return to those of both the broad market and the auto industry. If we call r_I the industry return, then we first would estimate parameters a,b,c in the regression

$$r_{Ford} = a + br_M + cr_I + e$$

Given these estimates we would calculate Ford's firm-specific return as

$$r_{Ford} - [\ a + br_M + cr_I\ ].$$

This estimate of firm-specific news would measure the market's assessment of the potential profitability of Ford's new model.

21. The market may have anticipated even greater earnings. *Compared to prior expectations,* the announcement was a disappointment.

22. Assumptions supporting passive management are

    a. frictionless markets (no transaction costs)

    b. informational efficiency

    c. primacy of diversification motives

    Active management is supported by the opposite assumptions, in particular, pockets of market inefficiency.

23. The low P/E effect and small size effect could be used to enhance portfolio performance *if* one could expect them to persist in the future. However, concentration in these stocks would lead

to departures from efficient diversification. In this case, beta would no longer be an adequate descriptor of portfolio risk because non-systematic risk would remain in the portfolio.

24. Reasons to avoid the strategy:

    a. You might believe that these effects will no longer work now that they are widely known.

    b. You might decide that too much diversification must be sacrificed to exploit these effects.

    c. The level of risk resulting from a low P/E, small capitalization emphasis might be inappropriate.

    d. You might decide that these "effects" are in fact a reward for bearing risk of a nature not fully captured by the beta of the stock. In other words, it may be that the abnormal returns on these strategies would not appear so high if we could more accurately risk-adjust performance.

25. a. The grandson is recommending taking advantage of (i) the small firm in January anomaly and (ii) the weekend anomaly.

    b. (i) Concentration of assets in stocks having very similar attributes may expose the portfolio to more risk than is desirable. The strategy limits diversification potential.
    (ii) Even if the study results are correct as described, each such study covers a specific time period. There is no assurance that future time periods would yield similar results.
    (iii) After the results of the studies became publicly known, investment decisions might nullify these relationships. If these firms in fact offered investment bargains, their prices may be bid up to reflect the now-known opportunity.

CHAPTER 13: BOND PRICES AND YIELDS

1. $\left(1 + \dfrac{BEY}{2}\right)^2 = 1 + EAY$

   $(1 + .12/2)^2 = 1.1236$

   $EAY = 12.36\%$

2. Since YTM exceeds current yield, the bond must offer "built-in" capital appreciation. Thereore, price is below par.

3. Since price is below par, the coupon rate, which equals coupon/par must be less than current yield, which equals coupon/price. Thus, coupon is less than 9%.

4. The effective annual yield on the semiannual coupon bond is 8.16%. If the annual coupon bonds are to sell at par they must offer the same yield, which will require an annual coupon of 8.16%.

5. The bond's YTM is 9.376%. Next year, when maturity is 9 years, the bond will sell for $859.70. Taxable income equals coupon plus built-in price appreciation because the bond is sold as an original-issue discount bond. Taxable income = 70 + (859.70 - 850) = $79.70.

6. If the effective annual yield is 21%, the semiannual rate is 10%. (Note that $1.10^2 = 1.21$). Therefore, the bond price is 70 PA(10%, 30) + 100 PF(10%, 30) = 717.19.

7. a. Effective annual rate on 3-month T-bill:

   $(\dfrac{100000}{97645})^4 - 1 = 1.02412^4 - 1 = .10$ or 10%

   b. Effective annual interest rate on coupon bond paying 5% semiannually:

   $(1.05)^2 - 1 = .1025$ or 10.25%

8. a. The bond pays $50 every 6 months

   Current price $50 x PA(4%, 6) + $1000 x PF(4%, 6) = $1052.42

   Assuming the market interest rate remains 4% per half year:

Price 6 months from now = $50 x PA(4%, 5) + $1000 x PF(4%, 5) = $1044.52

b. Rate of return $= \dfrac{\$50 + (\$1044.52 - \$1052.42)}{\$1052.42}$

$= \dfrac{\$50 - \$7.90}{\$1052.42} = \dfrac{\$42.10}{\$1052.42} = .04$ or 4% per six months.

9. Yield to maturity is 10%. Therefore price next year will be $\$1000/(1.10)^9 = \$424.10$.

Taxable income will be $424.10 - $385.54 = $38.56.

10. The original bond price is P = 2 PA(9%, 10) + 100 PF(9%, 10) = 55.076. The next year, only 9 years will remain until maturity, so price will be 58.033. Taxable income is 2 + (58.035 - 55.076) = $4.957.

11.

	Zero	8% coupon	10% coupon
a. Current prices	$463.19	$1000	$1134.20
b. Price 1 year from now	$500.25	$1000	$1124.94
Price increase	$ 37.06	$ 0.00	- 9.26
Coupon income	$ 0.00	$ 80.00	$ 100.00
Pre-tax income	$ 37.06	$ 80.00	$ 90.74
Pre-tax rate of return	8.00%	8.00%	$ 8.00%
Taxes*	$11.12	$24	$ 28.15
After-tax income	$25.94	$56	$ 62.59
After-tax return	5.60%	5.60%	5.52%
c. Price 1 year from now	$543.93	$1065.15	$1195.46
Price increase	$80.74	$65.15	$61.26
Coupon income	$0	$80	$100.00
Pre-tax income	$80.74	$145.15	$161.26
Pre-tax return	17.4%	14.5%	14.2%
Taxes	$24.22	$37.03	$42.25
After-tax income	$56.52	$108.12	$119.01
After-tax return	12.2%	10.8%	10.5%

* In computing taxes, we assume that the 10% coupon bond was issued at par and that the drop in price when the bond is sold at year end is treated as a capital loss and not as an offset to ordinary income.

12. The bond callable at 105 should sell at a lower price because the call provision is more valuable to the firm. Therefore, its YTM should be higher.

13. Lower. As time passes, the bond price, which now must be above par value, will approach par.

14. Factors which might make the PG debt more attractive to investors, therefore justifying a lower coupon yield, are:

   a. The PG debt has a shorter maturity. Given a normal yield curve, the shorter maturity implies less risk and commands a lower coupon.

   b. An option to extend the term for another 10 years is favorable if interest rates at that time are lower than today's. In contrast, if interest rates are rising, the investor can present the bond for payment and reinvest the money for better returns.

   c. In the event of trouble, the PG debt is a more senior claim. It has more underlying security in the form of a first claim against real property.

   d. The call feature is somewhat less onerous in the PG case as it provides three more years of call protection than the CLX issue. In addition, it provides a larger premium over par value if these bonds are called.

   e. The CLX bond has a sinking fund requiring CLX to retire $5 million per year of the face value of the issue. Since CLX has the option to retire this amount at the lower of par or market value, the sinking fund can work to the detriment of bondholders.

15. a. At least 9.20%, the yield to maturity of the current outstanding fixed rate issue.

    b. Floating rate notes may not sell at par for any of the following reasons:

       i. The yield spread between 6-month Treasury bills and other money market instruments of comparable maturity could be wider than when the bond was issued.

       ii. The credit standing of the firm may have eroded relative to Treasury securities which have no credit risk. Therefore, the 0.75 percent premium would become insufficient to sustain the issue at par.

iii. The coupon increases are implemented with a lag, i.e., once every six months. During a period of rising interest rates, even this brief lag will be reflected in the price of security.

c. The fixed rate bond is selling at $104.50 with a call price of $110. A fairly small decrease in rates could make it worthwhile to call the bond. Hence, call risk is moderate.

d. The fixed rate issue has the most appeal for an actively managed bond portfolio since a change in interest rates downward from present levels could produce a substantial gain in principal value in addition to the coupon interest. By contrast, floating rate notes lack significant capital gain or loss potential because the changing coupon interest tends to stabilize principal values: hence, the opportunity to maximize total return based on a forecast of declining interest rates is less than in the case of fixed rate obligations.

e. Yield to maturity incorporates the return from a fixed stream of coupon interest payments and the accretion of depreciation between the present price of the bond and its par value to be received at maturity. Because the floating rate note consists of a variable stream of interest payments to maturity, the effective maturity for comparative purposes with other debt securities is closer to next coupon reset date than the final maturity date. Therefore, yield-to-maturity is an indeterminable calculation for a floating rate note, with "yield-to-recoupon date" a more meaningful measure of total return.

16. a. Market conversion price = value if converted into stock

    = 12.882 x $66 = $850.21

b. Conversion premium = Bond price - value if converted into stock

    = $1020 - 12.882 x $66

    = $1020 - $850.21 = $169.79

    Conversion premium per share $= \dfrac{\$169.79}{12.882} = \$13.18$

c. Current yield $= \dfrac{\text{coupon}}{\text{price}} = \dfrac{\$72.50}{\$1020} = .0711$ or 7.11%

d. Dividend yield on common $= \dfrac{2.60}{66.00} = .0394$ or 3.94%

17. The 6% coupon bond is more attractive because its coupon rate is far below current market yields, and its price is far below the call price. Therefore, if yields do fall, the capital gains on the bond will not be limited by the call price. In contrast, the 14% bond can increase in value to at most $114, offering a maximum possible gain of less than 13%.

18. a. The 6% bond offers greater de facto call protection. Yields would need to fall greatly before it would be worthwhile to call the 6% bond, while the 9% bond is already in danger of call. The capital gains potential on the 6% coupon bond is far greater.

    b. The longer-term bond offers greater capital gains potential. Price is more sensitive to changes in yields.

19. (d) The Euless, Texas, General Obligation Bond, which has been refunded and secured by U.S. Government bonds held in escrow, has as good a credit quality as the U.S. bonds backing it. Euless, Texas has issued new bond to refund this issue, and with the proceeds purchased U.S. Government bonds. They did this rather than simply retire the old bonds because the old bonds are not callable yet and because Euless gets to earn the rate on T-bonds while paying a lower rate on its own bonds.

    The University of Kansas Medical Center Bonds are insured by a body which is not backed by the taxing power of the U.S. Treasury and therefore do not have as high a credit quality as the Euless bonds.

    The other two bonds have indeterminate quality. Since both are bonds of small local governments they may be subject to significant risk. The Sumter, South Carolina, Water and Sewer Revenue Bond probably is less likely to default because the revenues from such essential services are more reliable than the general taxing power of Riley County, Kansas.

20. (b) Economic uncertainty increases the chances of default and therefore widens the spread between Treasury and BAA corporate bond yields.

21. (b) The dividends from the preferred stock are less secure than the interest from the bond.

22. (d)

23. (c)

24. (c)

25. (d)

26. (c) The yield on the callable bond must compensate the investor for the risk of call.

Choice (a) is wrong because although the owner of a callable bond receives a premium plus the principal in the event of a call, the interest rate at which he can reinvest will be low. The low interest rate which makes it profitable for the issuer to call the bond makes it a bad deal for the bond's holder.

Choice (b) is wrong because a bond is more apt to be called when interest rates are low. Only if rates are low will there be an interest saving, for the issuer.

27. (b) is the only correct choice.

(a) is wrong because the YTM exceeds the coupon rate when a bond sells at a discount and is less than the coupon rate when the bond sells at a premium.

(c) is wrong because adding the *average* annual capital gain rate to the current yield does not give the yield to maturity. For example, assume a 10-year bond with a 6% coupon rate and a YTM of 8% per year. Its price is $865.80. The average annual capital gain is equal to ($1000 -865.80)/10 years = $13.42 per year. Using this number results in an average capital gains rate per year of $13.42/$865.80 = 1.55%. The current coupon yield is $60/$865.80 = .0693 per year or 6.93%. Therefore, the "total yield" is 8.48% (=1.55% + 6.93%) which is greater than YTM.

(d) is wrong because YTM is based on the assumption that any payments received are reinvested at the YTM and not at the coupon rate.

28. $(1+.12/4)^4 = 1.1255$. Choice (c) is correct.

29. (c)

30. (c)

CHAPTER 14: THE TERM STRUCTURE OF INTEREST RATES

1. Expectations hypothesis.

   The yields on long-term bonds are geometric averages of present and expected future short rates. An upward sloping curve is explained by expected future short rates being higher than the current short rate. A downward-sloping yield curve implies expected future short rates are lower than the current short rate. Thus bonds of different maturities have different yields if expectations of future short rates are different from the current short rate.

   Liquidity preference hypothesis.

   Yields on long-term bonds are greater than the expected return from rolling-over short-term bonds in order to compensate investors in long-term bonds for bearing interest rate risk. Thus bonds of different maturities can have different yields even if expected future short rates are all equal to the current short rate. An upward sloping yield can be consistent even with expectations of falling short rates if liquidity premiums are high enough. If, however, the yield curve is downward sloping and liquidity premiums are assumed to be positive, then we can conclude that future short rates are expected to be lower than the current short rate.

   Segmentation hypothesis.

   This hypothesis would explain a sloping yield curve by an imbalance between supply and demand for bonds of different maturities. An upward sloping yield curve is evidence of supply pressure in the long-term market and demand pressure in the short-term market. According to the segmentation hypothesis expectations of future rates have little to do with the shape of the yield curve.

2. b. The long-term rate is an average of the anticipated short-term rates *and* the current short-term rate.

3. True. Under the expectations hypothesis, there are no risk premia built into bond prices. The only reason for long-term yields to exceed short-term yields is an expectation of higher short-term rates in the future.

4. Uncertain. Lower inflation will usually lead to lower nominal interest rates. Nevertheless, if the liquidity premium is sufficiently great, long-term yields may exceed short-term yields *despite* expectations of falling short rates.

5.

Maturity	Price	YTM	Forward Rates
1	$943.40	6.00%	
2	$898.47	5.50%	5.00% ($1.055^2/1.06 - 1$)
3	$847.62	5.67%	6.00% ($1.0567^3/1.055^2 - 1$)
4	$792.16	6.00%	7.00% ($1.06^4/1.0567^3 - 1$)

6. Expected price path of 4-year zero coupon bond is as follows. (We discount the face value by the appropriate sequence of forward rates implied by this year's yield curve.)

Beginning of Year	Expected Price	Expected Rate of Return
1	$792.16	6.00% (839.69/792.16 - 1)
2	$\dfrac{1000}{1.05 \times 1.06 \times 1.07} = 839.69$	5.00% (881.68/839.69 - 1)
3	$\dfrac{1000}{1.06 \times 1.07} = 881.68$	6.00% (934.58/881.68 - 1)
4	$\dfrac{1000}{1.07} = 934.58$	7.00% (1000/934.58 - 1)

7. The bond price is derived by discounting each payment by the interest-rate factors appropriate for that payment's maturity:

$$\text{Price} = \frac{80}{1.08} + \frac{80}{1.08 \times 1.10} + \frac{1080}{1.08 \times 1.10 \times 1.12}$$

$$= 74.07 + 67.34 + 811.69$$

$$= 953.10$$

Using our financial calculator we find the yield to maturity:

$$\text{YTM} = 9.89\%$$

Realized compound yield: First find the future value, FV, of reinvested coupons and principal:

$$\text{FV} = (80 \times 1.10 \times 1.12) + (80 \times 1.12) + 1080 = \$1268.16$$

Then find the rate, y, that makes the FV of the purchase price equal to $1268.16.

$$953.10(1 + y)^3 = 1268.16$$

$$y = 10\%$$

8. You should expect it to lie above the curve since the bond must offer a premium to investors to compensate them for the option granted to the issuer.

9. a. We obtain forward rates from the following table:

Maturity	YTM	Price	Forward rate	
1 year	10%	909.09		
2	11	811.62	12.01%	$(1.11^2/1.10 - 1)$
3	12	711.78	14.03%	$(1.12^3/1.11^2 - 1)$

b. We obtain next year's prices and yields by discounting each zero's face value at the forward rates for next year that we derived in part (a):

Maturity	Price	YTM
1 year	892.78 [= 1000/1.1201]	12.01%
2 years	782.93 [= 1000/(1.1201 x 1.1403)]	13.02%

Note that this year's upward sloping yield curve implies, according to the expectations hypothesis, a shift upward in next year's curve.

c. The 2-year zero will next year be a 1-year zero, and will therefore sell at $1000/1.1201 = $892.78. Similarly, the current 3-year zero will be a 2-year zero and will sell for $782.93.

Expected total rate of return:

2-year bond: $\dfrac{892.78}{811.62} - 1 = 1.1000$ or 10%

3-year bond: $\dfrac{782.93}{711.78} - 1 = 1.1000$ or 10%

d. The current price of the bond should equal the value of each payment times the present value of $1 to be received at the "maturity" of that payment. The present value schedule can be taken directly fom the prices of zero-coupon bonds calculated above.

$$
\begin{aligned}
\text{Current price} &= 120(.90909) + 120(.81162) + 1120(.71178) \\
&= 109.09 + 97.39 + 797.19 \\
&= \$1003.67
\end{aligned}
$$

Similarly, the expected prices of zeros in 1 year can be used to calculate the expected bond value at that time:

$$
\begin{aligned}
\text{Expected price 1 year from now} &= 120 \times .89278 + 1120 \times .78293 \\
&= 107.1336 + 876.8816 \\
&= \$984.02
\end{aligned}
$$

$$
\begin{aligned}
\text{Total expected rate of return} &= \frac{120 + (984.02 - 1003.67)}{1003.68} \\
\\
&= \frac{120 - 19.65}{1003.68} = .1000 \text{ or } 10\%
\end{aligned}
$$

10. a. A 3-year zero with face value $100 will sell today at a yield of 6% and a price of $100/1.06^3 = \$83.96$. Next year, the bond will have a two-year maturity, and therefore a yield of 6% (reading from next year's forecasted yield curve). The price will be $89.00, resulting in a holding period return of 6%.

b. The forward rates based on today's yield curve are as follows:

Year	Forward Rate	
2	6.01%	$(1.05^2/1.04 - 1)$
3	8.03%	$(1.06^3/1.05^2 - 1)$

Using the forward rates, the yield curve *next* year is forecast as:

Maturity	YTM	
1	6.01%	
2	7.01%	$[(1.0601 \times 1.0803)^{1/2} - 1]$

The market forecast is for a higher YTM on 2-year bonds than your forecast. Thus, the market predicts a lower price and lower rate of return.

11. a. $P = \dfrac{9}{1.07} + \dfrac{109}{(1.08)^2} = 101.86$

b. YTM = 7.957%, which is the solution to: $9 \, PA(y,2) + 100 \, PF(y,2) = 101.86$

c. The forward rate for next year derived from the zero-coupon yield curve is approximately 9%:

$$1 + f_2 = \dfrac{(1.08)^2}{1.07} = 1.0901 \text{ which implies } f_2 = 9.01\%.$$

Therefore, using an expected rate for next year of $r_2 = 9\%$, we find that the forecast bond price is

$$P = \dfrac{109}{1.09} = 100$$

d. If the liquidity premium is 1% then the forecast interest rate is :

$E(r_2) = f_2$ - liquidity premium = 9% - 1% = 8%

and you forecast the bond to sell at $\dfrac{109}{1.08} = 100.93.$

12. a. The current bond price is 85 x .9434 + 85 x .87352 + 1085 x .81637 = 1040.20 which implies a yield to maturity of 6.97% [since 85 x PA(6.97%, 3) + 1000 x PF(6.97%, 3) = 1040.20].

b. If next year, y = 8%, then the bond price will be 85 x PA(8%,2) + 1000 x PF(8%,2) = 1008.92, for a rate of return equal to [85 + (1008.92 - 1040.20)]/1040.20 = .0516 or 5.16%

13.

Year	Forward rate	PV of $1 received at period end	
1	5%	1/1.05	= $.9524
2	7%	1/(1.05)(1.07)	= .8901
3	8%	1/(1.05)(1.07)(1.08)	= .8241

a. Price = (60 x .9524) + (60 x .8901) + (1060 x .8241) = 984.10

b. $984.10 = 60 \times PA(y, 3) + 1000 \times PF(y, 3)$ which can be solved to show that $y = 6.60\%$

c.

Period	Payment Received at end of period	Will grow by a factor of	To a future value of
1	$ 60	(1.07) (1.08)	69.34
2	$ 60	(1.08)	64.80
3	$1060	1	1060.00
			1194.14

$$984.10 (1 + RCY)^3 = 1194.14$$

$$1 + RCY = \left(\frac{1194.14}{984.10}\right)^{1/3} = 1.0666$$

$$RCY = 6.66\%$$

d. Next year, the bond will sell for

$60\ PA(7\%, 2) + 1000\ PF(7\%, 2) = 981.92$ for a capital loss of $984.10 - 981.92 = \$2.18$.

The holding period return is $\dfrac{60 + (-2.18)}{984.10} = .0587$ or 5.87%

14. a. The return on the one-year bond will be 6.1%. The price of the 4-year zero today is $\$1000/1.064^4 = \$780.25$. Next year, if the yield curve is unchanged, the bond will have a 3-year maturity, a YTM of 6.3%, and therefore sell for $\$1000/1.063^3 = \$832.53$, resulting in a one-year return of 6.7%. The longer-term bond gave the higher return in this case because its YTM fell during the holding period.

b. If you believed in the expectations theory, you could not believe that the yield curve next year will be the same as today's curve. The upward slope in today's curve would be evidence that expected short rates are rising and that the yield curve will shift upward, reducing the holding period return on the four-year bond. Under the expectations hypothesis, all bonds have equal expected holding period returns. Therefore, you would predict that the HPR for the 4-year bond would be 6.1%, the same as for the 1-year bond.

15.

Year	(1) CF received at year end	(2) Compound interest factor for each payment	(3) Future value of CF (1) x (2)
1	140	$(1.10)^2(1.08)^2$	197.59
2	140	$(1.10)(1.08)^2$	179.63
3	140	$(1.08)^2$	163.30
4	140	1.08	151.20
5	140	1	140.00

Total accumulation from coupons paid: 831.72

Principal at maturity of bond: 1000.00

Total at 5-year maturity: 1831.72

Initial cost of bond = 1000. Therefore, we find realized compound yield by solving

$$1000(1+y)^5 = 1831.72$$
$$y = 12.87\%$$

CHAPTER 15: FIXED INCOME PORTFOLIO MANAGEMENT

1. The percentage bond price change will be

$$- \text{Duration} \times \frac{\Delta y}{1+y} = -7.194 \times \frac{.005}{1.10} = -.0327 \text{ or a } 3.27\% \text{ decline.}$$

2. Computation of duration:

    a. YTM = 6%

(1) Time Until Payment (in years)	(2) Payment	(3) Payment Discounted at 6%	(4) Weight of each Payment	(5) Column (1) × Column (4)
1	60	56.60	0566	.0566
2	60	53.40	.0534	.1068
3	1060	890.00	.8900	2.6700
Column Sum		1000.00	1.0000	2.8334

Duration = 2.833 years

    b. YTM = 10%

(1) Time Until Payment (in years)	(2) Payment	(3) Payment Discounted at 10%	(4) Weight of each Payment	(5) Column (1) × Column (4)
1	60	54.55	.0606	.0606
2	60	49.59	.0551	.1102
3	1060	796.39	.8844	2.6532
Column Sum		900.53	1.0000	2.8240

Duration = 2.824 years, which is less than the duration at the YTM of 6%.

3. For a semiannual 6% coupon bond selling at par, we use parameters $c = 3\%$ per half-year period, $y = 3\%$, $T = 6$ semiannual periods. Using Rule 8, we find that

$$D = (1.03/.03) \, [\, 1 - (1/1.03)^6 \,]$$

$$= 5.58 \text{ half year periods}$$

$$= 2.79 \text{ years}$$

If the bond's yield is 10%, use Rule 7, setting the semiannual yield to 5%, and semiannual coupon to 3%.

$$D = \frac{1.05}{.05} - \frac{1.05 + 6(.03 - .05)}{.03[(1.05)^6 - 1] + .05}$$

$$= 21 - 15.448$$

$$= 5.552 \text{ half year periods}$$

$$= 2.776 \text{ years}$$

4. a. Bond B has a higher yield to maturity than bond A since its coupon payments and maturity are equal to those of A, while its price is lower. (Perhaps the yield is higher because of differences in credit risk.) Therefore, its duration must be shorter.

   b. Bond A has a lower yield and a lower coupon, both of which cause it to have a longer duration than B. Moreover, A cannot be called, which makes its maturity at least as long as that of B, which generally increases duration.

5.

t	CF	PV(CF)	Weight	w × t
1	10	9.09	.786	.786
5	4	2.48	.214	1.070
		11.57	1.0	1.856

   a. D = 1.856 years = required maturity of zero coupon bond

   b. Market value of zero must be $11.57 million, the same as the market value of the obligations. Therefore, the face value must be $11.57 x $(1.10)^{1.856}$ = $13.81 million.

6. C, D, A, B, E

7. Choose the longer-duration bond to benefit from a rate decrease.

   a. The Aaa-rated bond will have the lower yield to maturity and the longer duration.

   b. The lower-coupon bond will have the longer duration *and* more de facto call protection.

   c. Choose the lower coupon bond for its longer duration.

8. You should buy the 3-year bond because it will offer a 9% holding-period return over the next year. The 1-year bond would yield only 7%, and the two-year bond will experience a capital loss and will offer a one-year holding period return of less than 8%. Assuming that

the yields given in the question are appropriate for 8% coupon bonds, we would have the following prices and returns:

Maturity:	1 year	2 years	3 years
YTM at beginning of year	7%	8%	9%
Beginning of year prices	$1009.35	$1000.00	$974.69
Prices at year end (at 9% YTM)	$1000.00	$ 990.83	$982.41
Capital gain	-$ 9.35	-$ 9.17	$ 7.72
Coupon	$ 80.00	$ 80.00	$ 80.00
1-year total $ return	$ 70.65	$ 70.83	$ 87.72
1-year total rate of return	7%	7.08%	9%

The 3-year bond provides the greatest holding period return.

9.   a.   PV of the obligation = $10,000 x PA (8%, 2) = $17,832.65

The duration is 1.4808 years, which can be verified from rule 6 or a table like Table 15.3.

   b.   To immunize my obligation I need a zero-coupon bond maturing in 1.4808 years. Since the present value must be $17,832.65, the face value (i.e., the future redemption value) must be 17,832.65 x $1.08^{1.4808}$ or $19,985.26.

   c.   If the interest rate increases to 9%, the zero-coupon bond would fall in value to $\frac{\$19985.26}{1.09^{1.4808}}$ = $17,590.92 and the tuition obligation would fall to $17,591.11. The net position changes by only $.19.

If the interest rate falls to 7%, the zero-coupon bond would rise in value to $\frac{\$19985.26}{1.07^{1.4808}}$ = $18,079.99 and the tuition obligation would rise to $18,080.18. The net position changes by $.19.

The reason the net position changes at all is that as the interest rate changes so does the duration of the stream of tuition payments.

10.   The answer depends on the nature of the long-term assets which the corporation is holding. If those assets produce a return which varies with short-term interest rates then an interest-rate

swap would not be appropriate. If, however, the long-term assets are fixed-rate financial assets like fixed-rate mortgages then a swap might be risk-reducing. In such a case the corporation would swap its floating-rate bond liability for a fixed-rate long-term liability.

11. a. The duration of the perpetuity is 1.05/.05 = 21 years. Let w be the weight of the zero-coupon bond. Then we find w by solving:

$$w \times 5 \ + \ (1 - w) \times 21 = 10$$

$$21 - 16w = 10$$

$$w = 11/16 \text{ or } .6875$$

Therefore, your portfolio would be 11/16 invested in the zero and 5/16 in the perpetuity. Note that this assumes the YTM on the zero-coupon bond also is 5% per year.

b. The zero-coupon bond now will have a duration of 4 years while the perpetuity will still have a 21-year duration. To get a portfolio duration of 9 years, which is now the duration of the obligation, we again solve for w:

$$w \times 4 \ + \ (1 - w) \times 21 = 9$$

$$21 - 17w = 9$$

$$w = 12/17 \text{ or } .7059$$

So the proportion invested in the zero has to increase to 12/17 and the proportion in the perpetuity has to fall to 5/17.

12. a. From Rule 6, the duration of the annuity *if* it were to start in 1 year would be

$$\frac{1.10}{.10} \ - \ \frac{10}{(1.10)^{10} - 1} = 4.7255 \text{ years}$$

Because the payment stream starts in 5 years, instead of one year, we must add 4 years to the duration, resulting in duration of 8.7255 years.

b. The present value of the deferred annuity is 10,000 PA(10%, 10) / 1.10^4 = $41,968. Call w the weight of the portfolio in the 5-year zero. Then

$$5w + 20(1-w) = 8.7255$$

which implies that w = .7516 so that the investment in the 5-year zero equals

$$.7516 \times \$41,968 = \$31,543.$$

The investment in 20-year zeros is .2484 x $41,968 = $10,425.

These are the present of *market* values of each investment. The face values of each are the futures values of the investments.

The face value of the 5-year zeros is:

$$\$31,543 \times (1.10)^5 = \$50,800$$

meaning that between 50 and 51 zero coupon bonds, each of par value $1,000, would need to be purchased. Similarly, the face value of the 20-year zeros would be:

$$\$10,425 \times (1.10)^{20} = \$70,134.$$

13. a. The two risks are price risk and reinvestment rate risk. The former refers to bond price volatility as interest rates fluctuate, the latter to uncertainty in the rate at which coupon income can be reinvested.

b. Immunization means structuring a bond portfolio so that the value of the portfolio (with proceeds reinvested) will reach a given target level regardless of future changes in interest rates. This is accomplished by matching both the values and durations of the assets and liabilities of the plan. This may be viewed as a low risk bond management strategy.

c. Duration matching is superior to maturity matching because bonds of equal duration--not maturity--are equally sensitive to interest rate fluctuations.

d. Simply match the face value and maturity of the zero to the cash flow of the obligation. Zeros are ideal because they pose no issue of reinvestment rate risk.

e. Contingent immunization allows for active bond management unless and until the surplus funding in the account is eliminated because of investment losses. Contingent immunization allows for the possibility of above-market returns if the active management is successful.

14. The economic climate is one of impending interest rate increases. Hence, we will want to shorten portfolio duration.

    a. Choose the short maturity (1994) bond.

    b. The Arizona bond likely has lower duration. Coupons are about equal, but the Arizona yield is substantially higher.

    c. Choose the 15-3/8 coupon bond. Maturities are about equal, but its coupon is much higher, resulting in lower duration.

    d. The duration of the Shell bond will be lower if the effect of the higher yield to maturity and earlier start of sinking fund redemption dominates its slightly lower coupon rate.

    e. The floating rate bond has a duration that approximates the adjustment period, which is only 6 months.

15. a. This swap would have been made if the investor anticipated a decline long-term interest rates and an increase in long-term bond prices. The deeper discount, lower coupon 6-3/8% bond would provide more opportunity for capital gains, greater call protection, and greater protection against declining reinvestment rates at a cost of only a modest drop in yield.

    b. This swap was probably done by an investor who believed the 24 basis point spread in yield between the two bonds was too narrow, and if it widened to a more normal level, either a capital gain would be experienced on the Treasury note or a capital loss would be avoided on the Phone bond, or both. It could also have been done by an investor anticipating a decline in interest rates but who also wanted to maintain high current coupon income and have the better call protection of the Treasury note. The Treasury note would have unlimited potential for price appreciation in contrast to the Phone bond which would be restricted by its call price. Furthermore, if intermediate-term interest rates instead were to rise, the price decline of the higher quality, higher coupon Treasury note would likely be "cushioned" and the reinvestment return from the higher coupons would likely be greater.

c.	This swap would have been made if the investor were bearish on the bond market. The zero coupon note would be extremely vulnerable to an increase in interest rates since the yield to maturity, determined by the discount at the time of purchase, is locked in. This is in contrast to the floating rate note where interest is adjusted by formula each six months to reflect the current return available on six-month U.S. Treasury bills. The funds received in interest income on the floating rate notes could be used at a later time to purchase long-term bonds at more attractive yields.

d.	These two bonds are similar in most respects other than quality and yield. An investor who believed the yield spread between Government and Al bonds was too narrow would have made the swap either to take a capital gain on the Government bond or avoid a capital loss on the Al bond. The increase in call protection after the swap would not be a factor except under the most bullish interest rate scenarios. The swap does, however, extend maturity another 8 years and yield to maturity sacrifice is 169 basis points.

e.	The principal differences between these two bonds are the convertible feature of the Z mart bond and the yield and coupon advantage and longer maturity of the Lucky Ducks debentures. The swap would have been made if the investor believed some combination of the following: First, that the appreciation potential of the Z mart convertible, based primarily on the intrinsic value of Z mart common stock, was no longer as attractive as it had been. Second, that the yields on long-term bonds were at a cyclical high, causing bond portfolio managers who could take A2-risk bonds to reach for high yields and long maturities either to lock them in or take a capital gain when rates subsequently declined. Third, while waiting for rates to decline, the investor will enjoy an increase in coupon income. Basically, the investor is swapping an equity-equivalent for a long- term corporate bond.

CHAPTER 16: MACROECONOMIC AND INDUSTRY ANALYSIS

1. Expansionary (looser) monetary policy to lower interest rates would help stimulate investment and expenditures on consumer durables. Expansionary fiscal policy – lower taxes, higher government spending, increased welfare transfers – would stimulate aggregate demand directly.

2. a. Gold Mining. Gold traditionally is viewed as an inflation hedge. Loose monetary policy may lead to increased inflation, and thus could enhance the value of gold mining stocks.

   b. Construction. Loose monetary policy will lead to lower interest rates which ought to stimulate housing demand. The construction industry should benefit.

3. A depreciating dollar makes imported cars more expensive and American cars cheaper to foreign consumers. This should help the U.S. auto industry.

4. Supply side economists believe that a reduction in income tax rates will make workers more willing to work at current or even slightly lower (gross-of-tax) wages. Such an effect ought to mitigate cost pressures on the inflation rate.

5. a. The robotics process entails higher fixed costs and lower variable costs. This firm therefore will perform better in a boom and worse in a recession.

   b. Because it is more sensitive to the business cycle, the robotics firm will have the higher beta.

6. d

7. c

8. b

9. d

10. b or c. Eventually private investment will fall. Some argue that an initial temporary increase in private investment will occur if the increase in government spending initially stimulates the economy and increases consumer demand which then leads businesses to invest to increase capacity to meet that demand.

1. a. $k = D_1/P_0 + g$

    $.16 = 2/50 + g$

    $g = .12$

    b. $P_0 = D_1/(k - g) = 2/(.16 - .05) = 18.18$

    Initially, $P/E = 50/4 = 12.5$. After the forecast of g falls, $P/E = 18.18/4 = 4.55$.

2. a. $g = ROE \times b = 16 \times .5 = 8\%$

    $D_1 = \$2(1-b) = \$2(1 - .5) = \$1$

    $P_0 = D_1/(k-g) = \$1/(.12 - .08) = \$25$

    b. $P_3 = P_0(1+g)^3 = \$24(1.08)^3 = \$31.49$

3. a. $E(r) = k = \dfrac{D_1}{P_0} + g = \dfrac{.60}{20} + .08 = .11 = 11\%$

    b. The model assumes that the dividend growth rate is forever constant. Therefore, the model cannot be applied to firms that currently do not pay dividends. Second, the model is inappropriate when $g > k$ (which presumably cannot persist indefinitely). Third, the model cannot handle firms with variable dividend growth paths.

    c. One can use either P/E multiples or market-to-book multiples exhibited by other firms in the same industry.

4. a. $k = 6 + 1.25(14 - 6) = 16\%$; $g = 2/3 \times 9\% = 6\%$

    $D_1 = E_0 (1 + g) (1 - b) = 3(1.06) (1/3) = 1.06$

    $P_0 = \dfrac{D_1}{k - g} = \dfrac{1.06}{.16 - .06} = 10.60$

    b. Leading $P_0/E_1 = 10.60/3.18 = 3.33$

    Trailing $P_0/E_0 = 10.60/3 = 3.53$

    c. $PVGO = P_0 - \dfrac{EPS}{k} = 10.60 - \dfrac{3}{.16} = -8.15$

The low P/E ratios and negative PVGO are due to a poor ROE, 9%, that is less than the market capitalization rate, 16%.

d. Now, you revise b to 1/3, g to 1/3 x .09 = .03, and D_1 to E_0 (1.03)(2/3) = 2.06. Thus, V_0 = 2.06/(.16 - .03) = $15.85. V_0 increases because the firm pays out more earnings instead of reinvesting them at a poor ROE. This information is not yet known to the rest of the market.

5. Because beta = 1.0, k = market return, 15%. Therefore 15% = D_1/P_0 + g = 4% + g. Therefore g = 11%.

6. FI Corporation.

a. g = 5%; D_1 = $8; k = 10%
$$P_0 = \frac{D_1}{k - g} = \frac{\$8}{.10 - .05} = \$160$$

b. The dividend payout ratio is 8/12 = 2/3. The implied value of ROE on future investments is found by solving: g = b x ROE with g = 5% and b = 1/3. ROE = 15%.

c. The price assuming ROE = k is just EPS/k. P_0 = $12/.10 = $120. Therefore, the market is paying $40 per share ($160 - $120) for growth opportunities.

7. Three different valuation approaches for U.S. Tobacco Co.:

a. Balance sheet approaches: All of the asset related per share measures fall below the recent market price, and the stock therefore is not attractive on this basis:

Recent Price	$27.00
Book Value Per Share	6.42
Liquidation Value Per Share	4.90
Replacement Costs of Assets Per Share	9.15

b. Constant growth DDM approach: $V_0 = D_1/(k - g)$

$1.20/(.13 - .10) = $40

Thus intrinsic value exceeds market price, and the stock is attractive on this basis.

c. Earnings multiplier approach. If we apply the P/E multiplier of the S&P 500 to U.S. Tobacco's estimated EPS we get: 17.6 x $2.40 = $42.24. This exceeds UST's market price. Alternatively, if we use a P/E multiplier equal to l/k, in other words if we use the simple capitalized earnings approach, we get: l/k = 1/.13 = 7.6923. V_0 = $2.40 x 7.6923 = $18.46.

According to this approach, UST is overvalued and is not attractive.

8. High-Flyer stock.

a. $k = r_f + \beta (k_M - r_f) = .10 + 1.5(.15 - .10) = .10 + .075 = .175$, and $g = .05$. Therefore,

$$P_0 = \frac{D_1}{k - g} = \frac{\$2.50}{.175 - .05} = \frac{\$2.50}{.125} = \$20.$$

9.

	Stock A	B
Expected return on equity, ROE	14%	12%
Estimated earnings per share, E_1	$2.00	$1.65
Estimated dividends per share, D_1	$1.00	$1.00
Current market price per share, P_0	$27	$25
a. Dividend payout ratio, 1 - b	.5	.606
b. growth rate, g	7%	4.728%
c. intrinsic value, V_0	$33.33	$18.97

d. Stock A is the one you would invest in since its intrinsic value exceeds its price. You might want to sell short stock B.

10. Tennant Company

$D_0 = \$.96$ $E_0 = \$1.85$ $ROE = 1.85/13.07 = .141$

Dividend payout $= .96/1.85 = .519$

Plowback ratio $= b = .481$

$g = b \times ROE = .481 \times .141 = .0678$ per year.

$k = 7\% + 5\% = 12\%$ per year

a. $V_0 = \dfrac{D_1}{k - g} = \dfrac{.96(1.0678)}{.12 - .0678} = \$19.64$

b. If $ROE = 20\%$ and $b = .65$ then $g = 13\%$ per year, which is greater than k. Whenever $g >$ k, the constant growth rate DDM is meaningless since it gives a negative value for the value of the stock. You would therefore need to try a multistage DDM.

11. Nucor Corporation

Stock Price (Dec. 30, 1990)	$53.00
1990 Estimated Earnings	$ 4.25
1990 Estimated Book Value	$25.00
Indicated Dividend	$ 0.40
Beta	1.10
Risk-Free Return	7.0%
High Grade Corporate Bond Yield	9.0%
Risk Premium -- Stocks over Bonds	5.0%

a. The expected return on the stock market is the bond yield plus the risk premium of stocks over bonds: $E(r_M) = 9\% + 5\% = 14\%$

b. First we must calculate ROE in order to find g. ROE is the estimated EPS divided by estimated book value:

$ROE = 4.25/25 = 17\%$

Dividend payout $= .40/4.25 = .094$

$b = 1 - .094 = .906$

$g = b \times ROE = .906 \times 17\% = 15.4\%$ per year

Implied total return   = Dividend yield + g

$$= .40/53 + .154 = .0075 + .154$$

$$= .162 \text{ or } 16.2\% \text{ per year}$$

c.   Required return $r_f + \beta [E(r_M) - r_f] = 7\% + 1.1(14\% - 7\%) = 14.7\%$ per year

d.   Nucor's implied total return exceeds the required return using the CAPM. This suggests that its stock is undervalued, and it is an attractive investment.

12. <u>Nogro Corporation.</u>

   a. $P_0 = \$10$, $E_1 = \$2$, $b = .5$, $ROE = .2$

      $k = D_1/P_0 + g$

      $D_1 = .5 \times \$2 = \$1$

      $g = b \times ROE = .5 \times .2 = .1$

      Therefore, $k = \$1/\$10 + .1 = .1 + .1 = .2$ or 20%

   b.   Since k = ROE, the NPV of future investment opportunities is zero. Notice that

$$P_0 = \frac{EPS}{r} = \frac{\$2}{.20} = \$10$$

   c.   Since k = ROE, the stock price would be unaffected by cutting the dividend and investing the additional earnings. Similarly, eliminating dividends altogether should have no impact on the stock's price since the NPV of the investments would be zero.

13.   <u>Xyrong Corporation</u>

   a. $k = r_f + \beta[E(r_M) - r_f] = 8\% + 1.2(15\% - 8\%) = 16.4\%$

      $g = b \times ROE = .6 \times 20\% = 12\%$

$$V_0 = \frac{D_0(1 + g)}{k - g} = \frac{\$4 \times 1.12}{.164 - .12} = \$101.82$$

b. $P_1 = V_1 = V_0(1 + g) = 101.82 \times 1.12 = \$114.04$

$$E(r) = \frac{D_1 + P_1 - P_0}{P_0} = \frac{\$4.48 + \$114.04 - \$100}{\$100} = .1852 = 18.52\%$$

14. <u>DEQS Corporation.</u>

	0	1	5	6	. . .
E_t	10	12	24.883	\$29.860	
D_t	0	0	0	\$11.944	
b	1	1	1	.6	
g	.2	.2	.2	.09	

a. $P_5 = \dfrac{D_6}{k - g} = \dfrac{\$11.944}{.15 - .09} = \$199.07$

$P_0 = \dfrac{P_5}{(1 + k)^5} = \$98.97$

b. The price should rise by 15% per year until year 6: because there is no dividend, the entire return must be in capital gains.

c. It would have no effect since ROE = k.

15. <u>Duo Growth Co.</u>

	0	1	2	3	4	5	. . .
D_t	1	1.25	1.5625	1.953125			
g	.25	.25	.25	.05	. . . .		

a. The expected price 2 years from now is:

$P_2 = D_3 / (k - g) = 1.953125 / (.20 - .05) = \$13.02$

The PV of this expected price is $13.02 / 1.20^2 = \$9.04$

The PV of expected dividends in years 1 and 2 is:

$$\frac{D_1}{1.20} + \frac{D_2}{1.20^2} = \$2.13$$

Thus the current price should be $\$9.04 + \$2.13 = \$11.17$.

b. Expected dividend yield = D_1 / P_0 = 1.25/11.17 = .112 or 11.2%

c. The expected price one year from now is the PV of P_2 and D_2.

$P_1 = (D_2 + P_2) / 1.20 = (1.5625 + 13.02) / 1.20 = \$12.15.$

The implied capital gain is $(P_1 - P_0) / P_0$

$= (12.15 - 11.17) / 11.17 = .088$ or 8.8%

The implied capital gains rate and the expected dividend yield sum to the market capitalization rate. This is consistent with the DDM.

16. Generic Genetics (GG) Corporation.

	0	1	. . .	4	5
E_t	5	6		10.368	12.4416
D_t	0	0		0	12.4416

k = 15%

a. $P_4 = \dfrac{D_5}{k} = \dfrac{12.4416}{.15} = \$82.944$

$V_0 = \dfrac{P_4}{(1+k)^4} = \$47.42$

b. Its price should increase at a rate of 15% over the next year, so that the HPR will equal k.

17. MoMi Corporation.

	Projected Free Cash Flow in Year 1
Before-tax cash flow from operations	$2,100,000
Depreciation	210,000
Taxable Income	1,890,000
Taxes (@ 34%)	642,600
After-tax unlevered income	1,247,400
After-tax cash flow from operations (After-tax unlevered income + depreciation)	1,457,400
New investment (20% of cash flow from operations)	420,000
Free cash flow (After-tax cash flow from operations - new investment)	1,037,400

$k = 12\%$ Debt = $4 million

The value of the whole firm, debt plus equity, is

$$V_0 = \frac{C_1}{k\text{-}g} = \frac{\$1037400}{.12 - .05} = \$14,820,000$$

Since the value of the debt is $4 million, the value of the equity is $10,820,000.

18. <u>CPI Corporation.</u>

a. $k^* = D_1^* / P_0 + g^*$
$= 1/20 + .04 = .05 + .04 = .09$ or 9% per year.

b. Nominal capitalization rate:

$k = (1 + k^*) (1 + i) - 1$
$= 1.09 \times 1.06 - 1 = .1554$ or 15.54%

Nominal dividend yield:
$D_1/P_0 = 1 \times 1.06/20 = .053$ or 5.3%

Growth rate of nominal dividends:
$g = (1 + g^*) (1 + i) - 1$
$= 1.04 \times 1.06 - 1 = .1024$ or 10.24%

c. If expected real EPS are $1.80, then the estimate of intrinsic value using the simple capitalized earnings model is:
$V_0 = \$1.80 / .09 = \$20$

d. Inflating the EPS at a 6% rate gives EPS of $1.80 \times 1.06 = \$1.908$.
Capitalizing that at a nominal rate of 15.54%, gives an intrinsic value estimate of $12.28.

The conclusion is that to use the simple capitalized earnings valuation model the numerator should always be an estimate of real earnings and the denominator a real capitalization rate.

CHAPTER 18: FINANCIAL STATEMENT ANALYSIS

1. ROA = ROS x ATO. The only way that Crusty Pie can have an ROS higher than the industry average and an ROA equal to the industry average is for its ATO to be lower than the industry average.

2. ABC's ATO must be above the industry average.

3. ROE = (1 - tax rate)[ROA + (ROA - Interest rate)Debt/Equity]

   $ROE_A > ROE_B$

   Firms A and B have the same ROA. Assuming the same tax rate, they must have different interest rates and/or debt ratios.

4. c. Old plant and equipment is likely to have a low net book value, making the ratio of sales to net fixed assets higher.

5. b.

6. Seattle Manufacturing Corp.

   a. $$ROA = \frac{EBIT}{Assets} = \frac{Net\ income\ before\ tax + interest\ expense}{Average\ assets}$$

   $$= \frac{64.8 + 19.8}{.5(544.2 + 628)} = .144\ or\ 14.4\%$$

   b. $$EPS = \frac{Net\ income - preferred\ dividends}{Number\ of\ shares\ of\ common\ stock\ outstanding}$$

   Preferred dividends = .08 x $25 x 600,000 shares

   $$EPS = \frac{\$54.4\ million - \$1.2\ million}{.5(2.68\ million + 3\ million)\ shares} = \$18.73$$

c.   Acid test ratio $=$ $\dfrac{\text{Cash + commercial paper + receivables}}{\text{Current liabilities}}$

$$= \frac{\$6.6 + 15 + 93.2}{\$224.4} = .51$$

d.   Interest coverage ratio $= \dfrac{\text{EBIT}}{\text{Interest expense}}$

$$= \frac{\$64.8 + \$19.8}{\$19.8} = 4.3$$

e.   Receivables collection $= \dfrac{\text{Average receivables}}{\text{Sales}} \times 365$

period $= \dfrac{.5(77 + 93.2)}{1207.6} \times 365 = 25.7$ days

f.   Leverage ratio $= \dfrac{\text{Average assets}}{\text{Average common equity}}$

Common equity(1991) = $30 + 27 + 58.8 = \$115.8$ million

Common equity(1990) = $26.8 + 26.4 + 51 = \$104.2$ million

Leverage ratio $= \dfrac{.5(544.2 + 628)}{.5(104.2 + 115.8)} = 5.33$

7. Chicago Refrigerator Co.

a.   Quick Ratio $= \dfrac{\text{Cash + receivables}}{\text{Current liabilities}} = \dfrac{\$325 + \$3599}{\$3945} = .99$

b.   ROA $= \dfrac{\text{EBIT}}{\text{Assets}} = \dfrac{\text{Net income before tax + interest expense}}{\text{Average assets}}$

$$= \frac{\$2259 + 78}{.5(\$8058 + 4792)} = .364 \text{ or } 36.4\%$$

c. $\text{ROE} = \dfrac{\text{Net income - preferred dividends}}{\text{Average common equity}}$

Preferred dividends = .1 x $25 x 18,000 = $45,000

Common equity in 1991 = $829 + 575 + 1,949 = $3,353 million

Common equity in 1990 = $550 + 450 + 1,368 = $2,368 million

$$\text{ROE} = \dfrac{\text{Net income - preferred dividends}}{\text{Average common equity}} = \dfrac{\$1265 - 45}{.5(3353 + 2368)} = .426 \text{ or } 42.7\%$$

d. Earnings per share $= \dfrac{\$1265 - \$45}{829} = \$1.47 \text{ per share}$

e. Profit margin $= \dfrac{\text{EBIT}}{\text{Sales}} = \dfrac{\$2259 + 78}{\$12065} = .194 = 19.4\%$

f. Times interest earned $= \dfrac{\text{EBIT}}{\text{Interest expense}}$

$$= \dfrac{\$2259 + 78}{\$78} = 30$$

g. Inventory turnover $= \dfrac{\text{Cost of goods sold}}{\text{Average inventory}}$

$$= \dfrac{\$8048}{.5(1415 + 2423)}$$

h. Leverage ratio $= \dfrac{\text{Average assets}}{\text{Average common equity}}$

$$= \dfrac{.5(4792 + 8058)}{.5(2368 + 3353)} = 2.2$$

8. Atlas Corporation

    a. Acid test ratio $= \dfrac{\text{Cash + commercial paper + receivables}}{\text{Current liabilities}}$

        $= \dfrac{\$3.3 + 46.6}{112.2} = .44$

    b. Inventory turnover $= \dfrac{\text{Cost of goods sold}}{\text{Average inventory}}$

        $= \dfrac{\$475.6}{.5(125.6 + 143)} = 3.54$

    c. EPS $= \dfrac{\text{Net income - preferred dividends}}{\text{Number of shares of common stock outstanding}}$

        $= \dfrac{\$27.2}{.5(1.5 + 1.34)} = \$19.15$

    d. Interest coverage $= \dfrac{\text{EBIT}}{\text{Interest expense}}$

        $= \dfrac{\$32.4 + \$9.9}{\$9.9} = 4.27$

    e. Leverage ratio $= \dfrac{\text{Average assets}}{\text{Average common equity}}$

        $= \dfrac{.5(264.6 + 306.5)}{.5(52.1 + 57.9)} = 5.19$

9. a

10. a

11. a

12. b

13. d

14. c

15. c

16. c

17. b

18.

		1985	1989
(1) Operating margin =	$\dfrac{\text{Operating income - Depreciation}}{\text{Sales}}$	$\dfrac{38 - 3}{542} = 6.5\%$	$\dfrac{76 - 9}{979} = 6.8\%$
(2) Asset turnover =	$\dfrac{\text{Sales}}{\text{Total Assets}}$	$\dfrac{542}{245} = 2.21$	$\dfrac{979}{291} = 3.36$
(3) Interest Burden =	$\dfrac{\text{[Op Inc - Dep] - Int Expense}}{\text{Operating Income - Depreciation}}$	$\dfrac{38 - 3 - 3}{38 - 3} = .914$	1
(4) Financial Leverage	$\dfrac{\text{Total Assets}}{\text{Shareholders Equity}}$	$\dfrac{245}{159} = 1.54$	$\dfrac{291}{220} = 1.32$
(5) Tax rate =	$\dfrac{\text{Income taxes}}{\text{Pre-tax income}}$	$\dfrac{13}{32} = 40.63\%$	$\dfrac{37}{67} = 55.22\%$

Using the Dupont formula,

ROE = $[1 - (5)]$ x (3) x (1) x (2) x (4)

ROE(1985) = .5937 x .914 x .065 x 2.21 x 1.54 = .12 or 12%

ROE(1989) = .4478 x 1 x .068 x 3.36 x 1.32 = .135 or 13.5%

b. (i) Asset turnover measures the ability of a company to minimize the level of assets (current or fixed) to support its level of sales. The asset turnover increased substantially over the period, thus contributing to an increase in the ROE.

(ii) Financial leverage measures the amount of financing outside of equity including short and long-term debt. Financial leverage declined over the period thus adversely affected the ROE. Since asset turnover rose substantially more than financial leverage declined, the net effect was an increase in ROE.

1. In terms of dollar returns:

Stock price:	80	100	110	120
All stocks (100 shares)	8,000	10,000	11,000	12,000
All options (1000 shares)	0	0	10,000	20,000
Bills + options	9,360	9,360	10,360	11,360

In terms of rate of return, based on a $10,000 investment:

All stocks	-20%	0%	10%	20%
All options	-100%	-100%	0%	100%
Bills + options	-6.4%	-6.4%	3.6%	13.6%

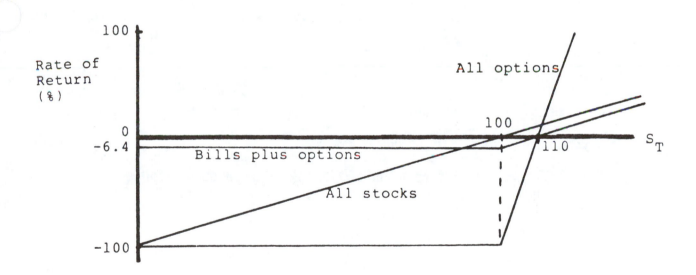

2. a. From put-call parity, $C - P = S - X/(1+r)^T$

$10 - P = 100 - 100/(1.10)^{1/4}$

$P = 10 - 100 + 100/(1.10)^{1/4} = \$7.645$

b. Purchase a straddle, i.e., both a put and a call on the stock. The total cost of the straddle would be $10 + 7.645 = \$17.645$, and this is the amount by which the stock would have to move in either direction for the profit on the call or put to cover the investment cost (not including time value of money considerations). Accounting for time value, the stock price would need to swing in either direction by $\$17.645 (1.1)^{1/4} = \$18.07$.

3. a. From put/call parity, $C = P + S - X/(1+r)^T$

$C = 4 + 50 - 50/(1.10)^{1/4} = 5.18$

b. Sell a straddle, i.e., sell a call *and* a put to realize premium income of $4 + $5.18 - $9.18. If the stock ends up at $50, both the options will be worthless and your profit will be $9.18. This is your maximum possible profit since at any other stock price, you will need to pay off on either the call or the put. The stock price can move by $9.18 in either direction before your profits become negative.

c. Buy the call, sell (write) the put, lend $50/(1.10)^{1/4}. The payoff is as follows:

Position	Initial Outlay	Final Payoff	
		$S_T \leq X$	$S_T > X$
Call (long)	$C = 5.18$	0	$S_T - 50$
Put (short)	$-P = 4.00$	$-(50 - S_T)$	0
Lending Position	$50/(1.10)^{1/4} = 48.82$	50	50
TOTAL	$C - P + \dfrac{50}{1.10^{1/4}} = 50$	S_T	S_T

By the put-call parity theorem, the initial outlay equals the stock price, S_o, or $50. In either scenario, you end up with the same payoff as you would if you bought the stock itself.

4. a. Selling now at $75 a share would raise $150,000. This sum invested at 10% per year (2.5% per quarter) would generate $3,750 for a total of $153,750 with no risk. It fully meets the goal of preserving the value of principal but offers no chance of reaching the $160,000 target.

   b. By writing covered call options, Melody takes in premium income of $4,000 which he can invest in CDs paying 10%. If the price of GM (P_{GM}) is less than or equal to $80 in March, Melody will have his stock plus the future value of the premiums $4,100. But the most he can have is $160,000 + $4,100 because the stock will be called away from him if P_{GM} exceeds $80. The payoff structure is:

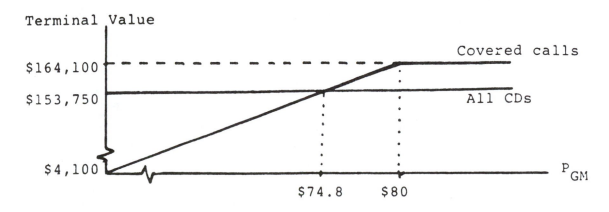

19-3

This strategy offers some extra premium income but leaves substantial downside risk. If P_{GM} fell to zero, Melody would be left with only $4,100. The strategy also puts a cap on the final value at $164,100, but this is more than sufficient to purchase the condo.

c. By buying put options at a $75 exercise price, Melody will be paying $4,000 in premiums to insure a minimum level for the final value of his position. Assuming he borrows the $4,000 at 10% per annum, he will have to repay $4,100 in March for this insurance. The payoff structure is:

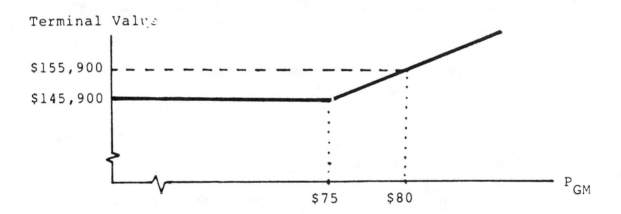

d. The net cost of the option position is zero. Payoff graph for holding GM stock, buying puts, and selling calls:

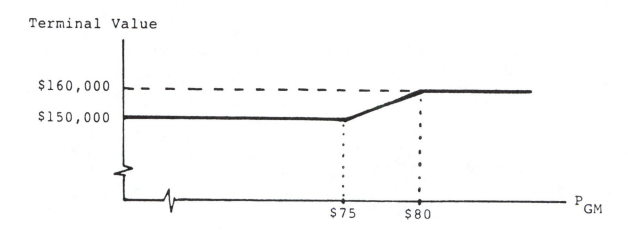

Terminal Value

If P_{GM} is less than or equal to $75, Melody has preserved the $150,000 in principal. If P_{GM} > $75, Melody gains up to a cap of $160,000, reached if P_{GM} ≥ $80.

Summary of Pay-offs

		Price of GM Stock		
	Minimum	$75	$80	Maximum
a. Switch to CDs	$153,750	$153,750	$153,750	$153,750
b. Covered calls	$ 4,100	$154,100	$164,100	$164,100
c. Protective Puts	$145,900	$145,900	$155,900	Unlimited
d. Buy Puts + Sell Calls	$150,000	$150,000	$160,000	$160,000

The appropriate ranking depends on how risk-averse Melody is and how likely he believes a fall or rise in the price of GM is. Strategy "a" offers no risk and would therefore be appropriate for the most risk-averse investor. Strategy "c" offers the best outcomes if GM stock rises to anything over $84.10 per share. Strategy "b" offers the best outcome if P_{GM} ends up in the vicinity of $75 to $84 per share.

The best strategy in this case would be (d) since it satisfies the two requirements of preserving the $150,000 in principal while offering a chance of getting $160,000. Our ranking would be   (1) d   (2) c   (3) a   (4) b.

5. a.

Outcome:	$S_T \leq X$	$S_T > X$
Stock	$S_T + D$	$S_T + D$
Put	$X - S_T$	0
Total	$X + D$	$S_T + D$

b.

Call	0	$S_T - X$
Zeros	$X + D$	$X + D$
Total	$X + D$	$S_T + D$

The total payoff of the two strategies are equal whether or not S_T exceeds X.

c. The stock-plus-put portfolio costs $S_0 + P$ to establish. The call-plus-zero portfolio costs $C + PV(X + D)$. Therefore,

$$S_0 + P = C + PV(X + D)$$

which is identical to equation 19.2.

6. a. Butterfly Spread

Position	$S < X_1$	$X_1 < S < X_2$	$X_2 < S < X_3$	$X_3 < S$
Long call (X_1)	0	$S - X_1$	$S - X_1$	$S - X_1$
Short 2 calls (X_2)	0	0	$-2(S - X_2)$	$-2(S - X_2)$
Long call (X_3)	0	0	0	$S - X_3$
Total	0	$S - X_1$	$2X_2 - X_1 - S$	$(X_2 - X_1) - (X_3 - X_2) = 0$

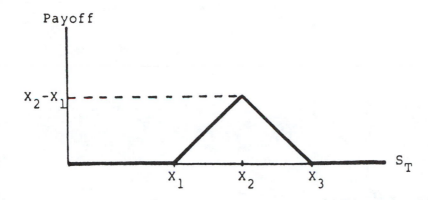

b. Vertical combination

Position	$S < X_1$	$X_1 < S < X_2$	$X_2 < S$
Long call (X_2)	0	0	$S - X_2$
Long Put (X_1)	$X_1 - S$	0	0
Total	$X_1 - S$	0	$S - X_2$

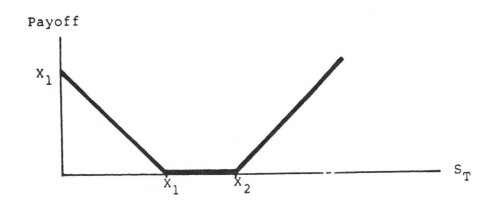

7. Bear spread

Position	$S < X_1$	$X_1 < S < X_2$	$X_2 < S$
Buy Call (X_2)	0	0	$S - X_2$
Sell Call (X_1)	0	$-(S - X_1)$	$-(S - X_1)$
Total	0	$X_1 - S$	$X_1 - X_2$

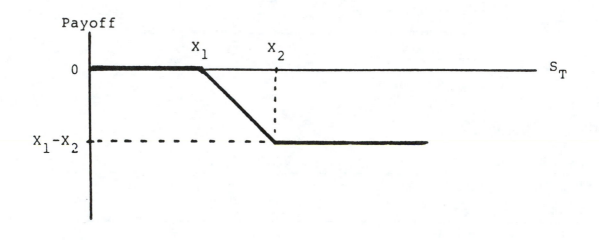

8. a.

Protective Put	$S_T \le 260$	$S_T > 260$
Stock	S_T	S_T
Put	$260 - S_T$	0
Total	260	S_T

Bills and Call	$S_T \le 280$	$S_T > 280$
Bills	280	280
Call	0	$S_T - 280$
Total	280	S_T

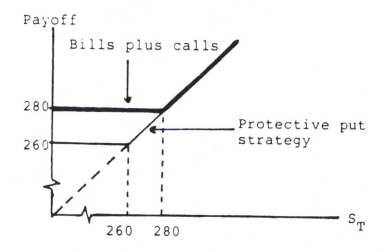

b. The bills plus call strategy has a greater payoff for some values of S_T and never a lower payoff. Since it's payoffs are always at least attractive, it must be more costly to purchase.

c. The initial cost of the stock plus put position is 302; that of the bills plus call position is 310.

	$S_T = 0$	$S_T = 260$	$S_T = 280$	$S_T = 300$
Stock	0	260	280	300
+Put	260	0	0	0
Payoff	260	260	280	300
Profit	-42	-42	-22	-2
Bill	280	280	280	280
+Call	0	0	0	20
Payoff	280	280	280	300
Profit	-30	-30	-30	-10

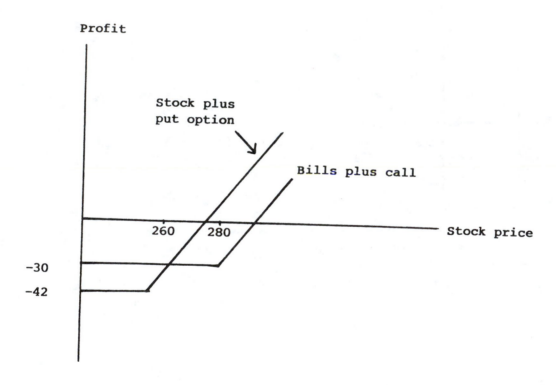

d. The stock plus put position does worse when the market is down, and better when the market is up. Its beta therefore is higher.

e. The exercise prices of the put and call options differ. Therefore, they should not satisfy the put-call parity relationship.

d. The stock and put strategy is riskier. It does worse when the market is down and better when the market is up. Therefore, its beta is higher.

e. Parity is not violated because these options have different exercise prices. Parity applies only to puts and calls with the same exercise price and expiration date.

9. The farmer has the option to sell the crop for a guaranteed minimum price to the government if the market price is too low. If the support price is denoted P_S and the market price P_m then the farmer has a put option to sell the crop (the asset) at an exercise price of P_S even if the price of the underlying asset, P, is less than P_S

10. The bondholders have in effect made a loan which requires repayment of B dollars, where B is the face value of bonds. If, however, the value of the firm, V, is less than B, the loan is satisfied by the bondholders taking over the firm. In this way, the bondholders are forced to "pay" B (in the sense that the loan is cancelled) in return for asset worth only V. It is as though the bondholders wrote a put on an asset worth V with exercise price B. Alternatively, one may view the bondholders as giving the right to the equityholders to reclaim the firm by paying off the B dollar debt. They've issued a call to the equity holders.

11. The executives get a bonus if the stock price exceeds a certain value and get nothing otherwise. This is the same as the payoff to a call option.

12. a.

	$S < 95$	$95 < S < 100$	$S > 100$
Written Call	0	0	- (S - 100)
Written Put	- (95 - S)	0	0
Total	S - 95	0	100 - S

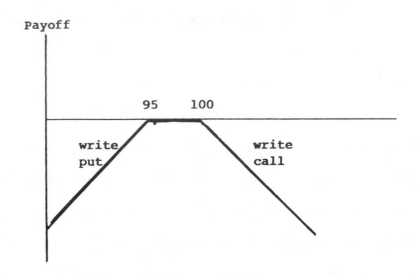

b. Proceeds from writing options:

Call =   3/8
Put =   6 1/4
Total = $6.625

If IBM sells at 97, both options expire out of the money, and profit = $6.625. If IBM sells at $110, the call written results in a cash outflow of $10 at maturity, and an overall loss of $3.375.

c. You break even when *either* the put *or* the call written results in a cash outflow of $6.625. For the put, this would require that 6.625 = 95 - S, or S = 88.375. For the call this would require that 6.625 = S - 100, or S = 106.625.

d. The investor is betting that IBM stock price will have low volatility. This position is similar to a straddle.

13. According to put-call parity (assuming no dividends), the present value of a payment of $90 can be calculated using the options with April maturity and exercise price of $90.

$$PV(X) = S + P - C$$
$$PV(90) = 89\ 5/8 + 2\ 7/8 - 2\ 11/16$$
$$= 89.625 + 2.875 - 2.6875$$
$$= 89.8125$$

14. a.b.

	$S < 100$	$100 < S < 110$	$S > 110$
Buy put (X=100)	100-S	0	0
Write put (X=110)	-(110-S)	-(110-S)	0
	- 10	S-110	0

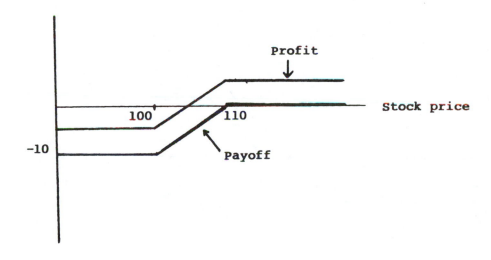

c. The value of this portfolio generally increases with the stock price. Its beta therefore is positive.

15. a. <u>Joe's strategy</u>

	Cost	Payoff S < 400	Payoff S > 400
Stock index	400	S	S
Put option (X=400)	20	400 - S	0
Total	420	400	S
Profit= payoff - 420		-20	S - 420

<u>Sally's Strategy</u>

	Cost	Payoff S < 390	Payoff S > 390
Stock index	400	S	S
Put option (X=390)	15	390 - S	0
Total	415	390	S
Profit = payoff - 415		-25	S - 415

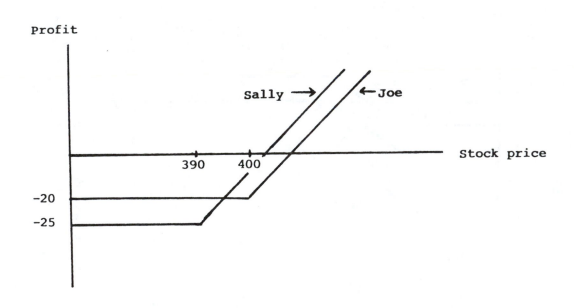

b. Sally does better when the stock price is high, but worse when the stock price is low. (The break-even point occurs at S = $395, when both positions provide losses of $20.)

c. Sally's strategy has greater systematic risk. Profits vary more sensitivity with the value of the stock index.

CHAPTER 20: OPTION VALUATION

1. Put values also must increase as the volatility of the underlying stock increases. We see this from the parity relation as follows:

   C = P + S - PV(X).

   Given a value of S and a risk-free interest rate, if C increases because of an increase in volatility, so must P to keep the parity equation in balance.

2. i. Put A must be written on the lower-priced stock. Otherwise, given the lower volatility of stock A, put A would sell for less than put B.

   ii. Put B must be written on the stock with lower price. This would explain its higher value.

   iii. Call B. Despite the higher price of stock B, call B is cheaper than call A. This can be explained by a lower time to expiration.

   iv. Call B. This would explain its higher price.

   v. Not enough information. The call with higher strike price also sells for less. This is consistent with either slightly higher or lower volatility.

3.

X	Hedge ratio
115	85/150 = .567
100	100/150 = . 667
75	125/150 = .833
50	150/150 = 1.000
25	150/150 = 1.000
10	150/150 = 1.000

4.

S	d_1	$N(d_1)$
45	-.0268	.4893
50	.5000	.6915
55	.9766	.8356

5. a. When S is 130, P will be 0.

    When S is 80, P will be 30.

    The hedge ratio is $(P_u - P_d)/(uS - dS) = (0 - 30)/(130 - 80) = -3/5$.

    b.
Riskless Portfolio	S = 80	S = 130
3 shares	240	390
5 puts	150	0
Total	390	390

    Present value $= 390/1.10 = 354.545$

    c. Portfolio cost $3S + 5P = 300 + 5P$, and is worth 354.545. Therefore P must be $54.545/5$

    $= \$10.91$.

6. The hedge ratio for the call is $(C_u - C_d)/(uS - dS) = (20-0)/(130 - 80) = 2/5$.

Riskless Portfolio	S = 80	S = 130
2 shares	160	260
5 calls written	0	0
Total	160	160

    $-5C + 200 = 160/1.10$. Therefore, $C = 10.91$.

    Does $P = C + PV(X) - S$?

    $10.91 = 10.91 + 110/1.10 - 100$

    $10.91 = 10.91$

7. $d_1 = .3182$ $N(d_1) = .6248$

    $d_2 = -.0354$ $N(d_2) = .4859$

    $Xe^{-rT} = 47.56$

    $C = 8.1316$

8. a. C falls to 5.5541

    b. C falls to 4.7911

    c. C falls to 6.0778

d. C rises to 11.5066

e. C rises to 8.7187

9. Less. The change in the call price would be $1 only if (i) there were 100% probability that the call would be exercised, and (ii) the interest rate were zero.

10. The correct answer depends on your interpretation of "holding all else equal." If you hold both the stock price and total volatility constant, beta is irrelevant to the option value. However, if you hold firm-specific risk constant, then higher beta implies higher total risk, so the option will be worth more.

11. Holding beta constant, the high firm-specific risk stock will have higher total volatility. The option will be worth more.

12. Lower. The option will be less in the money.

13. More. The option elasticity exceeds 1.0. In other words, the option is effectively a levered investment and will be more sensitive to interest rate swings.

14. It has increased. If not, the call price would have fallen.

15. Implied volatility is higher. If not, the put price would have fallen.

16. The hedge ratio approaches one. As S increases, the possibility of exercise approaches 1.0. $N(d_1)$ approaches 1.0.

17. Negative 1.0. As S falls, exercise becomes all but assured. $-[1 - N(d_1)]$ approaches -1, as $N(d_1)$ approaches 0.

18. The straddle hedge ratio is just the sum of the hedge ratios of each option. $.4 + (-0.5) = -0.1$.

19.

Put	X	Delta
A	10	-.1
B	20	-.5
C	30	-.9

20. A. Calls have higher elasticity than shares. For equal dollar investments, the call's capital gain potential will be higher than for stocks.

B. Calls have hedge ratios less than 1.0. For equal number of shares controlled, the dollar exposure of the calls is less than that of the stocks, and the profit potential is less.

21. S = 100; current value of portfolio

   X = 100; floor promised to clients (0% return)

   σ = .25; volatility

   r = .05; risk-free rate

   T = 4 years; horizon of program

   a. The put delta is $N(d_1) - 1 = .7422 - 1 = -.2578$

      Place 25.78% of the portfolio in bills, 74.22% in equity ($74.22 million)

   b. At the new portfolio value, the put delta becomes -.2779, meaning that $97 million x
      .2779 = $26.96 million should be in bills. The manager must sell an additional $1.176
      million of equity.

22. a.

Stock Price	Put Payoff
110	0
90	10

   The hedge ratio is -0.5. A portfolio comprised of one share and two puts would provide a
   guaranteed payoff of 110, with present value 110/1.05 = 104.76. Therefore,

   S + 2P = 104.76

   100 + 2P = 104.76

   P = 2.38

   b. The protective put strategy = 1 share + 1 put = 100 + 2.38 = 102.38

   c. Our goal is a portfolio with the same exposure to the stock as the hypothetical protective
      put portfolio. As the put's hedge ratio is -0.5, we want to hold 1 - 0.5 = 0.5 shares of
      stock, placing our remaining funds ($52.38) in bills, earning 5% interest.

Stock Price:	90	110
Half share	45	55
Bills	55	55
Total	100	110

This payoff is exactly the same as that of the protective put portfolio. Thus, the stock plus bills strategy replicates both the cost and payoff of the protective put.

23. When $r = 0$, one never should exercise a put early. There is no "time value cost" to waiting to exercise, but there is a "volatility benefit" from waiting. To show this more rigorously, consider this portfolio: lend $X and short one share of stock. The cost to establish the portfolio is $X - S_0$. The payoff at time T (with zero interest earnings on the loan) is $X - S_T$. In contrast, a put option has a payoff at time T of $X - S_T$ *if* that value is positive, and zero otherwise. The put's payoff is *at least* as large as the portfolio's, and therefore, the put must cost at least as much to purchase. Hence, $P \geq X - S_0$, and the put can be sold for more than the proceeds from immediate exercise. We conclude that it doesn't pay to exercise early.

24. a. Xe^{-rT}

    b. X

    c. 0

    d. 0

    e. It obviously is optimal to exercise immediately a put on a stock that has fallen to zero. The value of the American put equals the exercise price. Any delay in exercise lowers value by the time value of money.

25. a. <u>Step 1</u>: Calculate the option values at expiration. The two possible stock prices are $120 and $80. Therefore, the corresponding two possible call values are $20 and $0.

    <u>Step 2</u>: Find that the hedge ratio is $(20 - 0)/(120 - 80) = .5$. Therefore, form a riskless portfolio by buying one share of stock and writing two calls. The cost of the portfolio is $S - 2C = 100 - 2C$.

    <u>Step 3</u>: Show that the payoff of the riskless portfolio must equal $80. Therefore, find the value of the call by solving

$100 - 2C = $80/1.10

C = $13.636

b. The binomial option pricing model is a discrete version of the continuous time Black-Scholes option pricing model. As the number of intervals in the binomial model approaches infinity, the option value derived from this model approaches the value derived from the Black-Scholes model.

The binomial model is more flexible than the Black-Scholes model because it does not require one to assume constant interest rates and constant variance throughout the horizon. These values can be changed at any of the nodes in the binomial tree. However, the binomial model is more cumbersome to use since accuracy requires that the tree include many nodes.

26. The hedge ratio is (30-0)/(130 - 70) = .5. Form the riskless portfolio by buying one share of stock and writing two call options. The portfolio costs S - 2C = 100 - 2C. The payoff of the riskless portfolio is $70. Therefore, 100 - 2C = 70/1.10, which implies that C = $18.18, which is greater than the value in the lower-volatility scenario.

27. The hedge ratio for a put with X = 100 would be (0 - 20)/(120 - 80) = -.5. Form the riskless portfolio by buying one share of stock and buying two put options. The portfolio costs S + 2P = 100 + 2P. The payoff of the riskless portfolio is $120. Therefore, 100 + 2P = 120/1.10, which implies that P = $4.545. According to put-call parity, P + S = C + PV(X). Our estimates of option value satisfy this relationship: 4.545 + 100 = 13.636 + 100/1.10.

28. If one assumes that the only possible exercise date is just prior to the ex-dividend date, the relevant parameters for the Black-Scholes formula are:

$S_0 = 60$

$X = 55$

$T = 2$ months

$r = .5\%$ per month

sigma $= 7\%$

In this case, $C = \$6.04$.

If instead, one precommits to foregoing early exercise, one must reduce the stock price by the present value of the dividends. Therefore, we use

$S_0 = 60 - 2e^{-(.005 \times 2)} = 58.02$

$X = 55$

$T = 3$ months

$r = .5\%$ per month

sigma $= 7\%$

In this case, $C = \$5.05$. The pseudo-American value is the higher of these two values, $6.04.

29. True. The call option has an elasticity greater than 1.0. The call's percentage returns therefore are greater than those of the underlying stock. Hence the GM calls will respond more than proportionately when the GM stock price changes along with broad market movements. The beta of the GM calls therefore is greater than the beta of GM stock.

30. The elasticity of a call option is higher the more out of the money is the option. Therefore, the call with the higher exercise price will respond more sensitively to changes in the market index. It will have the higher beta.

31. As the stock price increases, conversion becomes ever-more assured. The hedge ratio approaches 1.0. The convertible bond price will move one-for-one with changes in the price of the underlying stock.

CHAPTER 21: FUTURES MARKETS

1. a. The close price for the spot index was 383.63. The dollar value of stocks is thus $500 x 383.63 = $191,815. The closing futures price for the June contract was 384.35, which has a dollar value of 384.35 x $500 = $192,175 which requires a margin of $19,217.50.

    b. The credit to your margin account would be $5.65 x 500 - $2,825, which is a percent gain of 2,825/19,217.50 - 14.7%. Note that the futures price itself increased only by 1.47%.

    c. Following the reasoning in part (b), any change in F is magnified by a ratio of l/(margin requirement). This is the leverage effect. The return will be -10%.

2. There is little hedging demand for cement futures since it is a small component of a typical individual's consumption basket. There is little speculative demand for cement futures, since cement prices are fairly stable and predictable.

3. The ability to buy on margin is one advantage of futures. Another is the ease of altering one's holdings of the asset. This is especially important if one is dealing in commodities, for which the futures market is far more liquid than the spot market.

4. Short selling results in an immediate cash inflow, whereas the short futures position does not:

Action	Initial CF	Final CF
Short Sale	$+P_0$	$-P_T$
Short Futures	0	$F_0 - P_T$

5. a. False. For any given level of the stock index, the futures price will be lower when the dividend yield is higher. This follows from spot-futures parity : $F_0 = S_0(1 + r - d)^T$.

    b. False. The parity relationship tells us that the futures price is determined by the stock price, the interest rate, and the dividend yield; it is *not* a function of beta.

    c. True. The short futures position will profit when the market falls. This is a negative beta position.

6. a. $F = S_0(1 + r) = 150 (1.08) = 162$

   b. $F = S_0(1 + r)^3 = 150 (1.08)^3 = 188.96$

   c. $F = 150(1.12)^3 = 210.74$

7. As S increases, so will F. You should buy the futures. Longing futures is better than buying the stock since you get the advantage of buying on margin.

8. a. Take a short position in T-bond futures, to offset interest rate risk. If rates increase, the loss on the bond will be offset by gains on the futures.

   b. Again, a short position in T-bond futures will offset the bond price risk.

   c. You wish to protect your cash outlay when the bond is purchased. If bond prices increase you will need an extra source of cash to purchase the bond with the anticipated contribution. Thus, you want a long futures position that will generate a profit if prices increase.

9. $F = S_0(1 + r - d) = 350(1 + .08 - .05) = 360.50$

10. According to parity relation the fair price for December futures is:

    $F_{Dec} = F_{June}(1 + r)^{1/2} = 346.30(1.08)^{1/2} = 359.89.$

    The actual futures price for December is too high relative to the June price. You should short the December contract and long the June contract.

11. a. $120(1.06) = 127.20$

    b. The stock price falls to $120(1 - .03) = 116.40$

       The futures price falls to $116.4(1.06) = 123.384$

       The investor loses $(127.20 - 123.384) \times 1000 = \$3816$. The margin account will be reduced by this amount.

    c. The percentage loss is $3816/12000 = 31.8\%$

12. a. The hedge works because any decrease in the price at which the bond can be sold because of an increase in market interest rates will be offset by gains on a short position in GNMA futures.

b. i. Yields on corporate bonds and GNMA passthroughs may not move in perfect

alignment.

ii. Taxes must be paid on the futures gains or losses.

iii. The yield curve may shift in a non-parallel manner, making duration calculations

suspect.

iv. Changes in GNMA prepayment rates may alter the GNMA duration.

13. The important distinction between a futures contract and an options contract is that the futures contract is an obligation. When an investor purchases or sells a futures contract, the investor has an obligation to accept or deliver, respectively, the underlying commodity on the expiration date. In contrast, the buyer of an option contract is not obligated to accept or deliver the underlying commodity but instead has the right, or choice, to accept or deliver the underlying commodity anytime during the life of the contract. Futures and options modify a portfolio's risk in different ways. Buying or selling a futures contract affects a portfolio's upside risk and downside risk by a similar magnitude. This is commonly referred to as symmetrical impact. On the other hand, the addition of a call or put option to a portfolio does not affect a portfolio's upside risk and downside risk to a similar magnitude. Unlike futures contracts, the impact of options on the risk profile of a portfolio is asymmetrical.

14. The parity value of F is $350 (1 + .07 - .04) = $360.50. The actual futures price is $370, too

high by $9.50.

Arbitrage Portfolio	CF now	CF in 1 year
Buy index	-350	$S_T + (.04 \times 350)$
Short futures	0	$370 - S_T$
Borrow	350	-350 (1.07)
Total	0	9.50

15. a. The parity condition for bond futures would simply reflect the fact that bond income is

derived from coupons instead of dividends. The current yield on the bonds (coupon

divided by price) plays the role of the dividend yield.

b. When the yield curve is upward sloping, the current yield will exceed the short rate.

Hence, distant futures prices will be lower than near-term futures prices.

16.a.

Action	Cash Flows Now	T_1	T_2
Long futures with T_1 maturity	0	$P_1 - F(T_1)$	0
Short futures with T_2 maturity	0	0	$F(T_2) - P_2$
At T_1 buy asset. Sell at T_2	0	$-P_1$	$+P_2$
At T_1, borrow $F(T_1)$	0	$F(T_1)$	$-F(T_1)(1+r)^{(T_2 - T_1)}$
Total	0	0	$F(T_2) - F(T_1)(1+r)^{(T_2-T_1)}$

b. Since the T_2 cash flow is riskless and no net investment was made, any profits would represent an arbitrage opportunity.

c. The zero-profit no-arbitrage restriction implies that

$$F(T_2) = F(T_1) (1+r)^{(T_2-T_1)}$$

17. The futures price is the agreed-upon price for deferred delivery of the asset. If that price is fair, then the *value* of the agreement ought to be zero; that is, the contract will be a zero-NPV agreement for each trader.

18. Because long positions equal short positions, futures trading *must* entail a "canceling out" of bets on the asset. Moreover, no cash is exchanged at the inception of futures trading. Thus, there should be minimal impact on the spot market for the asset, and futures trading should not be expected to reduce capital available for other uses.

CHAPTER 22: FUTURES MARKETS: A CLOSER LOOK

1. a. 427.5(1.10) - 8 = 462.25

    b. 427.5(1.05) - 8 = 440.875

    c. The futures price is too low. Buy futures, short the index, and invest the proceeds of the short sale in T-bills.

	CF Now	CF in 6 months
Buy futures	0	S_T - 424
Short index	427.5	$-S_T$ - 8
Buy bills	-427.5	448.875
	0	16.875

    The arbitrage profit equals the mispricing of the contract.

2. a. The value of the underlying stock is 500 x 450 = $225,000.

    $25/225,000 = .00011 = .011% of the value of the stock.

    b. 40 x .00011 = $.0044, less than half of one cent.

    c. .30/.0044 = 68.

3. a. Call p the fraction of proceeds from the short sale to which we have access. Ignoring transaction costs, the lower bound on the futures price that precludes arbitrage is $S_0(1 + rp)$ - D, which is the usual parity value, except for the factor p. The factor p arises because only this fraction of the proceeds from the short sale can be invested in the risk-free asset. We can solve for p as follows: 400 (1 + .022p) - $4.80 = 401, which can be rearranged to show that p = .66.

    b. With p = .9, the no-arbitrage lower bound on the futures price is 400(1 + .022 x .9) - 4.80 = 403.12. The actual futures price is 401. The departure from the bound is therefore 2.12. This departure also equals the potential profit from an arbitrage strategy. The strategy is to short the stock, which currently sells at 400 [investor receives 90% of the proceeds, 360; the remainder, 40, remains in margin account until the short position is covered in 6 months], buy futures, and lend:

	CF Now	CF in 6 months
Buy futures	0	$S_T - 401$
Short stock	360	$40 - S_T - 4.80$
Lend	-360	$360(1.022) = 367.92$
Total	0	2.12

The profit is 2.12 x 500 per contract.

4. a. Short. If the stock value falls, you need futures profits to offset the loss.

   b. Each contract is for $500 times the index, currently valued at 400. Therefore, each contract controls $200,000 worth of stock, and to hedge a $4 million portfolio, you need $\frac{4000000}{200000} = 20$ contracts.

   c. Now your stock swings only .6 as much as the market index. Hence, you need .6 as many contracts as in (b): 0.6 x 20 = 12 contracts.

5. The dollar is depreciating relative to the Swiss franc. To induce investors to invest in the U.S., the U.S. interest rate must be higher.

6. a. From parity, $F_0 = 1.60 \times \frac{1.04}{1.08} = 1.54$.

   b. Suppose that $F_0 = \$1.58$/pound. Then dollars are relatively too cheap in the forward market, or equivalently, pounds are too expensive. Therefore, you should buy dollars (sell pounds) forward.

Action Now	CF in $	Action at period-end	CF in $
Sell 1 pound forward for $1.58	0	Unwind: Collect $1.58, deliver 1 pound	$1.58 - E_1$
Buy 1/1.08 pounds	-1.60/1.08 =-$1.481	Exchange one pound for E_1$	E_1$
Borrow $1.481	$1.481	Repay loan; U.S. interest rate = 4%	-$1.54
Total	0	Total	$.04

7. Borrowing in the U.S. offers 4%. Borrowing in the U.K. and covering interest rate risk with futures or forwards offers a rate of return of: $(1+r_{UK})F_0/E_0 = 1.08(1.58/1.60) = 1.0665$, or

6.65%. It appears to be advantageous to borrow in the U.S. where the rates are lower, and to lend in the U.K. An arbitrage strategy involves simultaneous lending and borrowing with the covering of any interest rate risk:

Action Now	CF in $	Action at period-end	CF in $
Lend 1 pound in U.K.	-$1.60	Be repaid, and exchange proceeds for dollars	$(1.08) E_1$
Borrow in U.S.	$1.60	Repay loan	$-1.60(1.04)$
Sell forward 1.08 pounds for $1.58 each	0	Unwind	$1.08 (1.58 - E_1)$
Total	0	Total	$.0424

8. Muni yields, which are below T-bond yields because of their tax-exempt status, are expected to close in on Treasury yields. Because yields and prices are inversely related, this means that muni prices will perform poorly compared to Treasuries. Therefore you should establish a spread position, buying Treasury-bond futures and selling municipal bond futures. The net bet on the general level of interest rates is approximately zero. You have simply made a bet on relative performances in the two sectors.

9. Salomon holds bonds worth $5.354 million. If the interest rate increases to 5.1% semiannually, the value of the unhedged bonds will fall to $100 million/$(1.051)^{60}$ = $5.056 million, a capital loss of $298,000. (Each bond with face value $1000 would fall in value from $53.54 to $50.56 for a capital loss per bond of $2.98.) The T-bonds to be delivered on the bond contract are worth $90.80 at the current 4.5% semiannual yield. If the yield increases to 4.6%, their value will fall by $1,685 to $89,115, a loss of $1685 per contract. Therefore, you need 298,000/1685 = 177 contracts held *short* to hedge.

10. $F_0 = S_0(1 + r)^T$

    $= 350 (1.10) = 385$

    If F = 390, you could earn arbitrage profits as follows:

	CF Now	CF in 1 year
Buy gold	-350	S_T
Short futures	0	$390 - S_T$
Borrow	350	-385
	0	5

The future price must be 385 in order for this arbitrage strategy to yield no profits.

11. Suppose first that corn is never stored across a harvest, and second that the quality of a harvest has nothing to do with the quality of past harvests. Under these circumstances, there is no link between the current price of corn and the expected future price of corn. The quantity of corn stored will fall to zero before the next harvest, and thus the quantity of corn and the price in a year will depend solely on the quantity of next year's harvest, which has nothing to do with this year's harvest.

If a bad harvest this year means a worse than average harvest in future years, then the futures prices will rise in response to this year's harvest, although presumably the two-year price will change by less than the one-year price. The same reasoning holds if corn is stored across the harvest. Next year's price is determined by the available supply at harvest time, which is the actual harvest plus the stored corn. A smaller harvest now means less stored corn for next year which can lead to higher prices.

12. The required rate of return on an asset with the same risk as corn is $1 + .5(1.8 - 1) = 1.4\%$. Thus, in the absence of storage costs, corn would have to sell for $2.75 \times (1.014)^3 = 2.867$. The future value of the 3 year's storage costs is $.03 \times FA(1\%, 3) = .091$, where FA stands for the future value factor of a level annuity with a given interest rate and number of payments. Thus, the expected price would have to be $2.867 + .091 = 2.958$ to induce storage. Don't store it.

13. Situation A. The market value of the portfolio to be hedged is $20 million. The market value of the bonds controlled by one futures contract is $63,330. *If* we were to equate the market

values of the portfolio and the futures contract, we would sell $20,000,000/63.330 = 315.806$ contracts. However, we must adjust this "naive" hedge ratio for the price volatility of the bond portfolio relative to the futures contract. Price volatilities will differ according to both the durations of the bonds and the yield volatility of the bonds. In this case, the yield volatilities may be assumed equal, because any yield spread between the Treasury portfolio and the Treasury bond underlying the futures contract is likely to be stable. However, the duration of the Treasury portfolio is lower than that of the futures price. Adjusting the naive hedge ratio for relative duration and relative yield volatility, we obtain the adjusted hedge position:

$$315.806 \times \frac{7.6}{8.0} \times 1.0 = 300 \text{ contracts}$$

Situation B. Here we need to hedge the purchase price of the bonds, and require a long hedge. The market value of the bonds to be purchased is $20 million x .93 = $18.6 million. The duration ratio is 7.2/8.0, and the relative yield volatility is 1.25. Therefore, the hedge requires the treasurer to go long in the following number of contracts:

$$\frac{18600000}{63330} \times \frac{7.2}{8.0} \times 1.25 = 330 \text{ contracts}$$

14. If the exchange of currencies were structured as 3 separate forward contracts, the forward prices would be:

Year	Forward exchange rate	x $1 million marks =	Number of dollars to be delivered
1	.65 x (1.05/1.08)		$.6319 million
2	.65 x (1.05/1.08)^2		$.6144 million
3	.65 x (1.05/1.08)^3		$.5973 million

Instead, we deliver the same number, F*, of dollars each year. The present value of this obligation is determined as follows:

$$F^* \times PA(5\%, 3) = \frac{.6319}{1.05} + \frac{.6144}{1.05^2} + \frac{.5973}{1.05^3} = 1.6751$$

F* equals $.6151 million per year

15. a. The swap rate moved in favor of firm ABC. It was supposed to receive 1 percent more per year than it could receive in the current swap market. Based on notional principal of $10 million, the loss is .01 x $10 million = $100,000 per year.

    b. The market value of that fixed annual loss is obtained by discounting at the current rate on 3-year obligations, 7%. The loss is 100,000 x PA(7%, 3) = $262,432.

    c. If ABC had become insolvent, XYZ would not be harmed. XYZ would be happy to see the swap agreement cancelled. However, the swap agreement ought to be treated as an asset of ABC when the firm is reorganized.

16. If one buys the cap and writes a floor, one reproduces a conventional swap, which is costless to enter. Therefore, the proceeds form writing the floor must be the same as from buying the cap, $0.30.

17. The firm receives a fixed rate that is 2% higher than the market rate. The extra payment of .02 x $10 million has present value equal to 200,000 x PA(5, 8%) = $798,542.

CHAPTER 23: THE THEORY OF ACTIVE PORTFOLIO MANAGEMENT

1. a. Define $R = r - r_f$. The following estimates can be computed from the given observations:

$$E(R_B) = 11.16 \qquad\qquad E(R_U) = 8.42$$

$$\sigma_B = 21.24 \qquad\qquad \sigma_U = 14.8$$

$$\rho = .75$$

Risk neutral investors would prefer The Bull Fund because its performance suggests a higher mean. Given the estimates of the variance of the series and the small number of observations, the difference in the averages is too small to determine the superiority of Bull with any confidence.

b. Using the reward to volatility (Sharpe) measure,

$$S_B = \frac{E(r_B)}{\sigma_B} = \frac{11.16}{21.24} = .5254$$

$$S_U = \frac{8.42}{14085} = .5670$$

the data suggests that the Unicorn Fund dominates for a risk averse investor.

c. The decision rule for the proportion to be invested in the risky asset, as given by the formula

$$y = \frac{R}{A\sigma^2}$$

maximizes a mean variance utility of the form, $U = E(r) - .5A\sigma^2$ for which Sharpe's measure is the appropriate criterion for the selection of optimal risky portfolios. In any event, an investor with $A = 3$ would invest

$$y_B = \frac{.1116}{3 \times .2124^2} = .8246$$

$$y_U = \frac{.0842}{3 \times .1485^2} = 1.2727$$

If the investor in question ($A = 3$) thought that the quality of performance of Unicorn as reflected in S_U would last, he would actually borrow in order to invest in Unicorn.

2. $\sigma = 5.5\% \qquad\qquad r_f = 1\%$

The value of a call option on \$1 of the equity portfolio, with an exercise price of $X = 1 + r_f$ is (see valuation formula in Chapter 19, substitute $S = 1.0$ for the value of the stock, $1 + r_f$ for the value of the exercise price, and recall that $\log(1 + y)$ is approximately equal to y, for small y):

$$C = 2N(\sigma/2) - 1$$

where $N(\sigma/2)$ is the cumulative standard normal density for the value of half the standard deviation of the equity portfolio.

$$C = 2N(.0275) - 1.$$

Interpolating from the standard normal table:

$$= 2[.5080 + .75(.5120 - .5080)] - 1$$

$$= 1.0220 - 1 = .0220$$

Hence the added value of a perfect timing strategy is 2.2% per month.

3. a. Using the relative frequencies to estimate the conditional probabilities P_1 and P_2 for timers A and B,

	Timer A	Timer B
P_1	78/135 = .58	86/135 = .64
P_2	57/92 = .62	50/92 = .54
$P^* = P_1 + P_2 - 1$	.20 >	.18

The data suggests that timer A is the better forecaster

   b. Using the following equation to value the imperfect timing services of A and B,

$$C(P^*) = C(P_1 + P_2 - 1)$$
$$C_A(P^*) = .2 \times 2.2 = .44\% \text{ per month}$$
$$C_B(P^*) = .18 \times 2.2 = .40\% \text{ per month}$$

Indeed, timer B's added value is greater by 4 bps per month.

4 a. Compute alphas for the 4 stocks:

$$\alpha_i = r_i - [r_f + \beta_i(r_M - r_f)]$$
$$\alpha_A = .20 - [.08 + 1.3(.16 - .08)] = 0.016$$
$$\alpha_B = .18 - [.08 + 1.8(.16 - .08)] = -0.044$$
$$\alpha_C = .17 - [.08 + 0.7(.16 - .08)] = 0.034$$
$$\alpha_D = .12 - [.08 + 1.0(.16 - .08)] = -0.040$$

Stocks A and C have a positive alpha, whereas stocks B and D a negative one. The variances

$$\sigma_e^2(A) = .3364 \qquad\qquad \sigma_e^2(C) = .36$$

$$\sigma_e^2(B) = .5041 \qquad\qquad \sigma_e^2(D) = .3025$$

b. To construct the optimal risky portfolio, we first need to determine the active portfolio. Using the Treynor-Black technique, we construct the active portfolio

	$\dfrac{\alpha}{\sigma_e^2}$	$\dfrac{\alpha / \sigma_e^2}{\Sigma \alpha / \sigma_e^2}$
A	.0476	-.6142
B	-.0873	1.1265
C	.0944	-1.2181
D	-.1322	1.7058
---------	---------	---------
	.0225	1.0000
	-.1000	

	-.0775	

Do not be discouraged by the fact that the positive alpha stocks get negative weights and vice versa. Because of the reversed signs, the entire position in the active portfolio will be negative, returning everything to good order. With these weights the forecast for the active portfolio is:

$$\alpha = -.6142 \times .016 + 1.1265 \times (-.044) - 1.2181 \times .034 + 1.7058 \times (-.04)$$

$$= -.169041$$

$$\beta = -.6142 \times 1.3 + 1.1265 \times 1.8 - 1.2181 \times .7 + 1.7058 \times 1$$
$$= 2.08237$$

The high beta (higher than any individual beta) results from the short position in relatively low beta stocks and long position in relatively high beta stocks.

$$\sigma_e^2 = (-.6142)^2.3364 + 1.1265^2 \times .5041 + (-1.2181)^2.36 + 1.7058^2 \times .3025$$

$$= 2.18096 \qquad (\sigma_e = 1.4768)$$

Here, again, the levered positions in the high σ_e stock (B), overcomes the diversification effect, and ends up with a high residual standard deviation. The optimal risky portfolio has a proportion w^* in the active portfolio as follows:

$$w_0 = \frac{\alpha / \sigma_e^2}{E(r_M) / \sigma_M^2} = \frac{-.169041 / 2.18906}{.08 / .23^2} = \frac{-.07751}{1.51229} = -.51252$$

The negative position is indicated as explained earlier.
The adjustment for beta is

$$w^* = \frac{w_0}{1 + (1 - \beta) w_0} = \frac{-.51252}{1 + (1 - 2\ 08237)(-.051252)} = -.04856$$

With this position, we really hold a positive position in each individual stock with positive alphas and vice versa. The position in the index portfolio is:

$$1 - (-.04856) = 1.04856$$

c. To calculate Sharpe's measure for the <u>optimal risky portfolio</u> we need the appraisal ratio for the <u>active portfolio</u> and Sharpe's measure for the <u>market portfolio</u>. The appraisal ratio of the active portfolio is:

$$A = \alpha / \sigma_e = -.169041/1.4768 = -.11446$$

and $\qquad$ $A^2 = .01310$

Hence, the square of Sharpe's measure, S, of the <u>optimized risky portfolio</u> is :

$$S^2 = S_M^2 + A^2 = \left(\frac{.08}{.23}\right)^2 + .0131 = .1341$$

and $\qquad$ $S = .3662$

Compare this to the markets Sharpe measure,

$$S_M = (.08/.23) = .3478$$

The difference is: $\Delta = .0184$.

Note that the moderate improvement in performance results from small position in A because of its large residual value.

d. To calculate the exact makeup of the <u>complete portfolio</u>, we first need the mean excess return of the optimal risky portfolio is and its variance:

$$E(R_p) = \alpha_p + \beta_p E(R_M)$$

$$= -.04856(-.169041) + [1.04856 + (-.04856)2.0837].08$$

$$= .084 \quad \text{or } 8.4\%$$

Its variance is:

$$\sigma_P^2 = \beta_P^2 \sigma_M^2 + \sigma_{e_P}^2$$

$$= - [1.04856 + (-.04856)2.0823]^2 \, .23 \, + (-.04856)^2 \, 2.18096$$

$$= .052628 \qquad (\sigma_P = .2294)$$

Therefore, the optimal position in this portfolio is:

$$y(A = 2.8) = .08/(2.8 \times .052628) = .5429$$

While with a passive strategy

$$y = .08/(2.8 \times .232) = .5401$$

that is a difference of .3%.

The final positions of the complete portfolio are:

M:	.5429x1.04856 =	.5677
A:	.5429(-.04856)(-.6142) =	.0162
B:	.5429(-.04856)(1.1265) =	-.0297
C:	.5429(-.04856)(-1.2181) =	.0321
D:	.5429(-.04856)(1.7058)=	-.0450
		.5413

that is, 54.13% in risky assets and 45.87% in the risk-free assets.

5.   If a manager is not allowed to sell short he will not be interested to include stocks with negative alphas in his portfolio, so that A and C are the only ones he will consider.

	α	σ_e^2	$\dfrac{\alpha}{\sigma_e^2}$	$\dfrac{\alpha / \sigma_e^2}{\Sigma \alpha / \sigma_e^2}$
A:	.016	.3364	.0476	.3352
C:	.034	.3600	.0944	.6648
			.1420	1.0000

The forecast for the active portfolio is:

$$\alpha = .3352 \times .016 + .6648 \times .034 = .02797$$

$$\beta = .3352 \text{ x } 1.3 + .6648 \text{ x } .7 = .90112$$

$$\sigma_e^2 = .3352^2 \text{ x } .3364 + .6648^2 \text{ x } .36 = .1969 \qquad (\sigma_e = .4437)$$

The active portfolio is:

$$w_0 = \frac{\alpha / \sigma_e^2}{E(r_M) / \sigma_M^2} = \frac{.02797 / .1969}{.08 / .23^2} = \frac{.14205}{1.51229} = .09393$$

and adjusting for beta

$$w^* = \frac{w_0}{1 + (1 - \beta) w_0} = \frac{.09393}{1 + (1 - .90112)(.09393)} = .09307$$

The appraisal ratio of the active portfolio is

$$A = \alpha / \sigma_e = .02797/.4437 = .06304$$

and hence, square of Sharpe's measure is:

$$s^2 = (08/23)^2 + .06304^2 = .12496$$

and $\qquad$ $S = .3535$

Relative to the market's Sharpe measure $S_M = .3478$, the difference is $\Delta = .0057$. This difference is smaller than the one we calculated in 4(c) when short sales are allowed, ($\Delta = .0184$).

The mean excess return of the optimal risky portfolio is:

$$E(R_p) = .09307 \text{ x } .02797 + .08(.90693 + .09307 \text{ x } .90112)$$

$$= .08187 \quad \text{or } 8.187\%$$

Its variance is:

$$\sigma_P^2 = .9307^2 \text{ x } .1969 + [.90693 + .09307 \text{ x } .90112]^2 .23^2$$

$$= .05364$$

and $\qquad$ $\sigma_P = .2316$

So that
$$y(A = 2.8) = .08187/(2.8 \times .05364) = .5451$$

which is more than the position in the superior, unconstrained portfolio.

b. The utility loss function for the three portfolios, the constrained (no short sales), the market and the unconstrained is:

$$U_C = .08187 \times .5451 - (1/2)2.8 \times .5451^2 \times .05364$$
$$= .0223$$

which is better than

$$U_M = .08 - (1/2)2.8 \times .23^2$$
$$= .00594$$

but less than

$$U_C(\text{unconstrained}) = .084 \times .5413 - (1/2)2.8 \times .5413^2 \times .052628$$
$$= .0239$$

The constrained portfolio is in between the market portfolio and the unconstrained portfolio

6. a. The optimal passive portfolio is obtained from equation 7.8 Chapter 7 on Optimal Risky Portfolios.

$$w_M = \frac{E(R_M)\sigma_H^2 - E(R_H)Cov(r_H,r_M)}{E(R_M)\sigma_H^2 + E(R_H)\sigma_M^2 - 2[E(R_H) + E(R_M)]Cov(r_H,r_M)}$$

where $R_M = .08$, $R_H = .02$ and $Cov(r_H,r_M) = \rho\sigma_M\sigma_H = .6 \times .23 \times .18 = .02484$

$$w_M = \frac{.08 \times .18^2 - .02 \times .02484}{.08 \times .18^2 + .02 \times .23^2 - (.08 + .02).02484} = 1.797$$

and
$$w_H = -.797$$

[This means that with no short sales, portfolio H would have to be left out of the passive portfolio.]

b. With short sales allowed,

$$E(R_{passive}) = 1.797 \times .08 + (-.797) \times .02 = .12782$$

$$\sigma^2_{passive} = (1.797 \times .23)^2 + [(-.797).18]^2 + 2 \times 1.797(-.797).02484$$

$$= .120254$$

$$\sigma_{passive} = .3468$$

Sharpe's measure in this case is:

$$S_{passive} = .3686$$

compared with the market's Sharpe measure of

$$S_M = .08/.23 = .3478$$

Thus, in terms of the Sharpe measure, the difference is: $\Delta = .0208$, which is an improvement of almost 6%.

c. The improvement of utility of the expanded model of H and M vs. a portfolio of M alone is calculated below.

$$y(A = 2.8) = .12782/(2.8 \times .120254) = .3796$$

So that

$$U_{passive} = .12782 \times .3896 - (1/2)2.8 \times .3796^2 \times .120254$$

$$= .0243$$

Compared with $U_M = .00594$ from problem 5.

7. The first step is to find the beta of the stocks relative to the optimized passive portfolio:

$$\beta_A = \frac{Cov(r_A, r_{passive})}{\sigma^2_{passive}}$$

$$= \frac{1.797 b_M \sigma^2_M - .797 b_H \sigma^2_H}{\sigma^2_{passive}}$$

$$= \frac{1.797 \times 1.2 \times .23^2 - .797 \times 1.8 \times .18^2}{.120254} = .5621$$

$$\beta_B = \frac{1.797 \times 1.4 \times .23^2 - .797 \times 1.1 \times .18^2}{.120254} = .8705$$

$$\beta_C = \frac{1.797 \times .5 \times .23^2 - .797 \times 1.5 \times .18^2}{.120254} = .07315$$

$$\beta_D = .7476$$

Now the alphas relative to the optimized portfolio are:

$$\alpha_A = .20 - .08 - .56210 \times .14376 = .03919$$
$$\alpha_B = .18 - .08 - .87050 \times .14376 = -.025143$$
$$\alpha_C = .17 - .08 - .07315 \times .14376 = .079484$$
$$\alpha_D = .12 - .08 - .74760 \times .14376 = -.067475$$

The residual variances are now obtained from:

$$\sigma_{e_A}^2 = \sigma_A^2 - \beta_{A_{passive}}^2 \times \sigma_{passive}^2$$

$$= .6525^2 - (.5621 \times .3468)^2 = .3878$$

$$\sigma_{e_B}^2 = .8219^2 - (.8705 \times .3468)^2 = .5844$$

$$\sigma_{e_C}^2 = .6212^2 - (.07315 \times .3468)^2 = .3852$$

$$\sigma_{e_D}^2 = .5962^2 - (.7476 \times .3468)^2 = .2882$$

From this point, the procedure is identical to that of problem 6.

	$\dfrac{\alpha}{\sigma_e^2}$	$\dfrac{\alpha / \sigma_e^2}{\Sigma \alpha / \sigma_e^2}$
A	.1011	3.3366
B	-.0430	-1.4191
C	.2063	6.8086
D	-.2341	-7.7261
	.0303	1.0000

The active portfolio parameters are:

$$\alpha = 3.3366 \times .03919 + (-1.4191)(-.02514) + 6.8086 \times .07948 + (-7.7261)(-.06747)$$

$$= 1.22894$$

$$\beta = 3.3366 \times .5621 + (-1.4191)(.8705) + 6.8086 \times .07315 + (-7.7261)(.7476)$$
$$= -4.6378$$

$$\sigma_e^2 = 3.3366^2 \times .3878 - (-1.4191)^2 .5844 + 6.8086^2 \times .3852 + (-7.7261^2).2882$$
$$= 40.5544$$

The proportions in the overall risky portfolio can now be determined.

$$w_0 = \frac{\alpha/\sigma_e^2}{E(r_{passive})/\sigma_{passive}^2} = \frac{1.22894/40.5544}{.12782/.120254} = \frac{.03030}{1.06292} = .02851$$

$$w^* = \frac{.02851}{1 + (1 + 4.6378).02535} = .0246$$

a. Sharpe's measure for the optimal risky portfolio with restrictions is derived from the following equation for S^2:

$$S^2 = S_{passive}^2 + (\alpha/\sigma_e)^2 = \frac{.12782^2}{.120254} + \frac{1.228945^2}{40.5544} = .1731$$

$$S = .4161$$

relative to

$$S_{passive} = \frac{.12782}{.34678} = .3686$$

The difference $\Delta = .0475$

b. The mean excess return of this portfolio is:

$$E(R) = .0246 \times 1.228045 + [.9721 + .0246 \times (-4.6378)].12782 = .1399$$

and its variance and standard deviation are:

$$\sigma^2 = [.9721 + .0246 \times (-4.6378)]^2 \times .120254 + .0246^2 \times 40.5544 = .11303$$

$$\sigma = .3363$$

So that the position in it would be:

$$y(A = 2.8) = \frac{.1399}{2.8 \times .11307} = .4247$$

c. The utility value for this portfolio is:

$$U = .4274 \times .1399 - (1/2)2.8 \times .4274^2 \times .11307 = .08833$$

Superior to all previous alternatives.

8. If short sales are not allowed, then the passive portfolio reverts to M, so the solution mimics the one in problem 7.

CHAPTER 24: PORTFOLIO PERFORMANCE EVALUATION

1. a. Arithmetic average: $r_{ABC} = 10\%$ $r_{XYZ} = 10\%$

    b. Dispersion: $\sigma_{ABC} = 7.45\%$ $\sigma_{XYZ} = 14.9\%$

    XYZ has a greater dispersion

    c. Geometric average:

    $r_{ABC} = (1.2 \times 1.1 \times 1.14 \times 1.05 \times 1.01)^{1/5} - 1 = 9.80\%$

    $r_{XYZ} = (1.3 \times 1.1 \times 1.18 \times 1.0 \times .92)^{1/5} - 1 = 9.19\%$

    Despite the equal arithmetic averages, XYZ has a lower geometric average. The reason is

    that the greater variance of XYZ drives the geometric mean further below the arithmetic

    mean.

    d. In terms of "forward looking" statistics, the arithmetic mean is the better estimate of

    exprected return. Therefore, if the data reflect the probability of *future* returns, 10 percent

    is the expected return of *both* stocks.

2. a. Time-weighted average ignores portfolio cash flows.

Year	Return [(capital gains + dividend)/price]
1991-1992	[(110-100)+4]/100 = 14%
1992-1993	[(90-110)+4]/110 = -14.55%
1993-1994	[(95 - 90)+4]/90 = 10%

    Arithmetic mean: 3.15%

    Geometric mean: 2.33%

time	Cash flow	Explanation
0	-300	Purchase of three shares at $100 each.
1	-208	Purchase of two shares at 110 less dividend income on three shares held.
2	110	Dividends on five shares plus sale of one share at price of $90 each.
3	396	Dividends on four shares plus sale of four shares at price of $95 each.

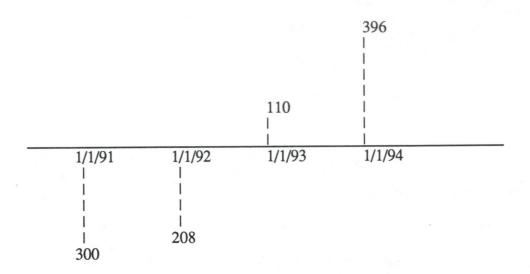

Dollar-weighted return = Internal rate of return = -.1661%.

3. a.

	E(r)	σ	β
Stock A	11	10	.8
Stock B	14	31	1.5
Market index	12	20	1.0
Risk-free asset	6	0	0

The alphas for the two stocks are:

$\alpha_A = 11 - [6 + .8(12 - 6)] = .2\%$

$\alpha_B = 14 - [6 + 1.5(12 - 6)] = -1\%$

Ideally you would want to take some long position in A and short position in B.

b. If you will hold only one of the two stocks, then the Sharpe measure is the appropriate criterion:

$$S_A = \frac{11 - 6}{10} = .5$$

$$S_B = \frac{14 - 6}{31} = .26$$

A is preferred using the Sharpe criterion.

4. a.

	Portfolio A	Portfolio B
(i) Alpha is the intercept of the regression	1%	2%
(ii) Appraisal ratio. $\alpha/\sigma(e)$	.097	.1047
(iii) Sharpe measure $(r_p - r_f)/\sigma$	.406	.337
(iv) Treynor measure $(r_p - r_f)/\beta$	.08833	.105

b. (i)   If this is the only risky asset, then Sharpe's measure is the one to use. A's is higher so it is better.

(ii) If it is mixed with the index fund, the contribution to the *overall* Sharpe measure is determined by the appraisal ratio; therefore, B is preferred.

(iii) If it is one of many portfolios then Treynor's measure counts and B is better.

5.

	Selection Ability	Timing Ability
a.	Bad	Good
b.	Good	Good
c.	Good	Bad
d.	Bad	Bad

6. a. Bogey: .60 x 2.5% + .30 x 1.2% + .10 x 0.5% = 1.91%
      Actual: .70 x 2.0% + .20 x 1.0% + .10 x 0.5% = 1.65%
      *Under*performance: .26%

   b. *Security Selection*

Market	Excess return within market	Portfolio weight	Contribution to performance = (1) × (2)
Equity	-0.5%	.70	-0.35%
Bonds	-0.2%	.20	-0.04%
Cash	0	.10	0
Contribution of security selection			-0.39%

   c. *Asset Allocation*

Market	Excess weight in market	Index return minus bogey	Contribution to performance = (1) × (2)
Equity	.10	0.59%	.059%
Bonds	- .10	-0.71	.071
Cash	0	0	0
Contribution of asset allocation			.13 %

   Summary

Security selection	- .39%
Asset allocation	.13%
Excess performance	- .26%

7. Support: A manager could be a better forecaster in one type of circumstance. Contradict: Although the above argument is possible, it is quite unlikely. To the extent that observing a manager over an entire cycle increases the number of observations, it would improve the reliability of the measurement. If we adequately control for exposure to the market, then market performance should not affect relative performance of individual managers.

8. It does, to some degree, if those manager groups can be made sufficiently homogeneous with respect to style.

9. a. The manager's alpha is 10 - [6 + .5(14 - 6)] = 0

b. From Black-Jensen-Scholes and others, we know that on average, portfolios with low beta have had positive alphas. Therefore, given the manager's low beta, performance could be sub-par despite the estimated alpha of zero.

10. a. $\alpha_A = 24 - [12 + 1.0(21 - 12)] = 3\%$

   $\alpha_B = 30 - [12 + 1.5(21 - 12)] = 4.5\%$

   $T_A = (24 - 12)/1 = 12$

   $T_B = (30 - 12)/1.5 = 12$

   As an addition to a passive diversified portfolio, both A and B are candidates because they have positive alphas.

   b. (i) The funds may have been trying to time the market. In that case, the SCL of the funds may be non-linear.

   (ii) One year's worth of data is too small a sample.

   (iii) The funds may have significantly different levels of diversification. If both have the same risk-adjusted return, the fund with the less diversified portfolio has a higher exposure to risk because of its higher non-diversifiable risk. Since the above measure adjusts for systematic risk only, it does not tell the entire story.

11. a. Indeed, the one year results were terrible, but one year is a poor statistical base on which to draw inferences. Moreover, this fund was told to adopt a long-term horizon. The Board specifically instructed the investment manager to give priority to long term results.

   b. The sample of pension funds had a much larger share in equities compared to Alpine's. Equities performed much better than bonds. Yet Alpine was told to hold down risk, investing at most 25% of its assets in common stocks. (Alpine's beta was also somewhat defensive).

   c. Alpine's alpha measures its risk-adjusted performance compared to the market's.
   $\alpha = 13.3 - [7.5 + .9(13.8 - 7.5)] = .13\%$, actually above zero.

   d. Note that the last 5 years, particularly the last one, have been bad for bonds, the asset class that Alpine had been encouraged to hold. Within this asset class, however, Alpine did much better than index funds (bottom two lines). Moreover, despite the fact that the bond index underperformed both the actuarial return and T-bills, Alpine outperformed both. Alpine's performance *within* each asset class has been superior on a risk-adjusted basis. Its overall disappointing returns were due to a heavy asset allocation weighting towards bonds, which was the Board's – not Alpine's – choice.

e. A trustee may not care about the time weighted return, but that return is more indicative of the manager's performance. After all, the manager has no control over the cash inflow of the fund.

12. Method I does nothing to separate the effects of timing versus security selection decisions. It also uses a very questionable "neutral position," the composition of the portfolio at the beginning of the year.

Method II is not perfect, but is the best of the three techniques. It at least tries to focus on market timing by examining the returns on portfolios constructed from bond market *indexes* using actual weights in various indexes versus year-average weights. The problem with the method is that the year-average weights need not correspond to a client's "neutral" weights. For example, what if the manager were optimistic over the whole year regarding long-term bonds? Her average weighting could reflect her optimism, and not a neutral position.

Method III uses net purchases of bonds as a signal of bond manager optimism. But such net purchases can be due to withdrawals or contributions to the fund rather than the manager's decisions. (Note that this is an open-ended mutual fund.) Therefore, it is inappropriate to evaluate the manager based on whether net purchases turn out to be reliable bullish or bearish signals.

13. b

14. b

15. c

16. a

17. c

18. b

19. b

20. d

CHAPTER 25: HEDGING

1. If the beta of the portfolio were 1.0, she would sell $1 million of the index. Because beta is 1.25, she needs to sell $1.25 million of the index

2. She must sell $1 million x $\frac{8}{10}$ = $.8 million of T-bonds.

3. The farmer must sell forward 100,000 bushels x (1/.90) = 111,111 bushels of yellow corn. This requires selling 111,111/5,000 = 22.2 contracts.

4. Suppose the yield on your portfolio increases by 1.5 basis points. Then the yield on the T-bond contract is likely to increase by 1 basis point. The loss on your portfolio will be $1 million x Δy x D^* = $1 million x .00015 x 4 = $600. The change in the futures price (per $100 par value) will be $95 x .0001 x 9 = $.0855, or on a $100,000 par value contract, $85.50. Therefore you should sell $600/$85.50 = 7 contracts.

5. Both the bond and the contract may be considered as selling at par value since the bond coupon will be chosen to result in a bond price of par. If yield changes on the bond and the contracts are each 1 basis point, the bond value will change by

$$\$10 \text{ million x } .0001 \text{ x } 8 = \$8000.$$

The contract will result in a cash flow of

$$\$100,000 \text{ x } .0001 \text{ x } 6 = \$60.$$

Therefore, you should sell 8000/60 = 133 contracts. You *sell* because you need profits on the contract to offset losses as a bond issuer if interest rates increase.

6. a. 400 (1.01) = 404

   b. $8 million/(500 x 400) = 40 contracts *short*.

   c. 40 x 500 x (404 - S_T) = 8,080,000 - 20,000 S_T

   d. The expected return on a stock is

   $$\alpha + r_f + \beta \ [E(r_M) - r_f].$$

   The CAPM predicts that α = 0. In this case, however, if you believe that

α = 2% (or .02), you forecast a portfolio return of

$$.02 + .01 + 1.0(r_M - .01)$$

$$= .03 + 1 \times (r_M - .01).$$

e. The expected rate of return on the portfolio also can be written as

$$.03 + 1 \times [(S_T/400 - 1) - .01].$$

The *dollar* value of the stock portfolio as a function of the market index is therefore

$$\$8 \text{ million } [.03 + S_T/400 - 1 - .01]$$

$$= \$160,000 + 20,000 \, S_T$$

The dollar value of the short futures position will be (from part c)

$$8,080,000 - 20,000 \, S_T$$

The total value of the portfolio plus the futures proceeds is therefore

$$160,000 + 20,000 \, S_T$$
$$\underline{+ \, 8,080,000 - 20,000 \, S_T}$$
$$8,240,000$$

The payoff is independent of the value of the stock index. Systematic risk has been eliminated by hedging (although firm-specific risk remains).

f. The portfolio-plus-futures position cost $8 million to establish. The expected end-of-period value is $8,240,000. The rate of return is therefore 3 percent.

g. The beta of the hedged position is 0. The fair return should be $r_f = 1\%$. Therefore, the alpha of the position is 3% - 1% = 2%, the same as the alpha of the portfolio. Now, however, one can take a position on the alpha without incurring systematic risk.

7. You would short $.50 of the market index contract and $.75 of the computer industry stock for each dollar held in IBM.

8. Using a volatility of 32% and time to maturity T = .25 years, the hedge ratio for Exxon is $N(d_1)$ = .5567. Because you believe the calls are underpriced (selling at too low implied volatility), you will buy calls and short .5567 shares for each call that you buy.

9. The calls are cheap (implied $\sigma = .30$) and the puts are expensive (implied $\sigma = .34$). Therefore, buy calls and sell puts. Using the "true" volatility of $\sigma = .32$, the call delta is .5567 and the put delta is $.5567 - 1 = -.4433$. Therefore buy $.5567/.4433 = 1.256$ puts for each call purchased.

10. Although people will want to hedge this source of risk, the lack of correlation between security returns and the risk factor will make such hedging impossible. Because security returns are uncorrelated with the risk factor, the securities cannot serve to offset the uncertainty surrounding that factor. Hence there is no reason for investors to tilt their portfolios toward or away from any security for hedging in connection with the factor.

11. a. The stock is a good inflation hedge. Its real return increases when the inflation rate increases. This will offset the exposure I already suffer due to my fixed-income pension.

    b. If I produce gold and already benefit from inflation, I do not want this stock for hedging. It exaggerates my current exposure.

    c. If retirees are more numerous, there will be a net hedging demand for stocks with high inflation betas that will drive up their prices and reduce their expected rates of return.

12. a. The industry factor is a statistically useful means to describe returns because it helps to explain movement in a nontrivial group of stocks. It is a common factor for all machine tool producers. However, there is no compelling reason to identify this industry return with a significant extramarket hedge factor. Investors can diversify away "industry-specific" risk if each industry is sufficiently small. On this score, a machine-tool factor would not be expected to appear in connection with the multifactor CAPM.

    b. One would not expect the factor to command a risk premium. In the jargon of the APT, it would be a nonpriced factor. The industry factor would not be expected to command a risk premium by the usual principles of the CAPM, since industry-specific risk presumably can be diversified away. Neither does it seem that the machine-tool industry portfolio is a natural hedge for any significant source of extramarket risk. More generally, the APT allows for many factors (such as industry co-movements) that help to describe returns of various subsets of securities, but that do not serve to hedge a meaningful source of systematic risk.

13. Method 1: Sell short T-bonds to offset risk of P&G bonds. To determine how many T-bonds to sell, use the hedge ratio, which gives the ratio of the number of T-bonds to sell for each P&G bond held in portfolio.

The yield beta tells us how much the P&G bond yield changes in relation to the yield on the T-bond. The regression equation indicates that the yield beta is 0.89, indicating that P&G yields are somewhat more stable than Treasury yields.

The hedge ratio is therefore

$$.89 \times \frac{.08286}{.08766} = .8413$$

Since Byron holds 10,000 P&G bonds ($10 million face value), he needs to sell short .8413 x 10,000 Treasury bonds, each with face value $1000.

Method 2: Sell T-bond futures contracts. Here, the yield beta is .47 so the hedge ratio is

$$.47 \times \frac{.08286}{.0902} = .4318$$

Byron needs to sell short .4318 of the benchmark T-bonds on which the contract is written for each P&G bond he holds. This means he needs to sell 4,318 bonds. Since each futures contract calls for delivery of 100 bonds (i.e., $100,000 face value), he would need to short 43.18 contracts.

A more advanced answer that goes beyond the material covered in the text would note that the actual delivery bond is not the benchmark 8% coupon bond. Since the conversion factor of the "cheapest to deliver" is 1.1257 the hedge ratio is increased to

$$4.318 \times 1.1257 = 48.6 \text{ contracts}$$

CHAPTER 26: INTERNATIONAL AND EXTENDED DIVERSIFICATION

1. a. $10,000/2 = 5,000$ pounds

   $5,000/40 = 125$ shares

   b. To fill in the table, we use the relation:

   $$1 + r_{US} = (1 + r_{UK}) E_1/E_0$$

Price per Share (Pounds)	Pound-Denominated Return (%)	Dollar-Denominated Return (%) For Year-End Exchange Rate		
		1.80	2.00	2.20
35	-12.5	-21.25	-12.5	-3.75
40	0	-10.00	0	10.00
45	12.5	1.25	12.5	23.75

   c. The dollar-denominated return equals the pound-denominated return in the scenario that the exchange rate remains unchanged over the year.

2. The standard deviation of the pound-denominated return (using 3 degrees of freedom) is 10.21%. The dollar-denominated return has a standard deviation of 13.10% (using 9 degrees of freedom), greater than the pound standard deviation. This is due to the addition of exchange rate risk.

3. First we calculate the dollar value of the 125 shares of stock in each scenario. Then we will add the profits from the forward contract in each scenario.

	Dollar Value of Stock at given exchange rate		
Exchange Rate:	1.80	2.00	2.20
Share Price in Pounds			
35	7,875	8,750	9,625
40	9,000	10,000	11,000
45	10,125	11,250	12,375
Profits on Forward Exchange: [$= 5000(2.10 - E_1)$]	1,500	500	-500

	Total Dollar Proceeds at given exchange rate		
Exchange Rate:	1.80	2.00	2.20
Share Price in Pounds			
35	9,375	9,250	9,125
40	10,500	10,500	10,500
45	11,625	11,750	11,875

Finally, calculate the dollar-denominated rate of return, recalling that the initial investment was $10,000.

	Rate of return (%) for given exchange rate		
Exchange Rate:	1.80	2.00	2.20
Share Price in Pounds			
35	-6.25	-7.50	-8.75
40	5.00	5.00	5.00
45	16.25	17.50	18.75

b. The standard deviation is now 10.24%. This is lower than the unhedged dollar-denominated standard deviation.

4. Currency Selection

EAFE: $[.30 \times (-10\%)] + (.10 \times 0) + (.60 \times 10\%) = 3\%$

Manager: $[.35 \times (-10\%)] + (.15 \times 0) + (.50 \times 10\%) = 1.5\%$

Loss of 1.5% relative to EAFE.

Country Selection

EAFE: $(.30 \times 20) + (.10 \times 15) + (.60 \times 25) = 22.5\%$

Manager: $(.35 \times 20) + (.15 \times 15) + (.50 \times 25) = 21.75\%$

Loss of 0.75% relative to EAFE

Stock Selection

$(18 - 20) \times .35 + (20 - 15) \times .15 + (20 - 25) \times .50 = -2.45\%$

Loss of 2.45% relative to EAFE.

5. $1 + r_{US} = (1 + r_{UK})F/E_0 = 1.08 \times 1.85/1.75 = 1.1417$, implying $r_{US} = 14.17\%$.

6. You can now purchase $10,000/1.75 = 5,714.29$ pounds, which will grow with 8% interest to 6,171.43 pounds. Therefore, to lock in your return, you need to sell forward 6,171.43 pounds at the forward exchange rate.

7.

Portfolio	Average Return	Standard Deviation
All REITs	22.26%	19.71%
All T-bonds	7.91%	11.50%
50% REITs/ 50% bonds*	15.09%	13.08%

*Standard deviation = $[.5^2 \times 19.71^2 + .5^2 \times 11.50^2 + 2 \times .5 \times .5 \times 19.71 \times 11.50 \times .36]^{1/2}$

11. a. The primary rationale is the opportunity for diversification. Factors that contribute to low correlations of stock returns across national boundaries are:

   i. imperfect correlation of business cycles

   ii. imperfect correlation of interest rates

   iii. imperfect correlation of inflation rates

   iv. exchange rate volatility

   b. Obstacles to international investing are:

   i. Availability of information, including insufficient data on which to base investment decisions Interpreting and evaluating data that is different in form and/or content than the routinely available and widely understood U.S. data is difficult. Much foreign data also is reported with a considerable lag.

   ii. Liquidity, in terms of the ability to buy or sell, in size and in a timely manner, without affecting the market price. Most foreign exchanges offer (relative to U.S. norms) limited trading and involve greater price volatility. Moreover, only a (relatively) small number of individual foreign stocks enjoy comparable-to-U.S. liquidity, although this drawback is improving steadily.

   iii. Transaction costs, particularly when viewed as a combination of commission plus spread plus market impact costs, are well above U.S. levels in most foreign markets. This, of course, adversely affects return realization from the outset.

   iv. Political risk.

   v. Foreign currency risk, although this can be largely hedged.

c. The asset-class performance data for this particular period reveal that non-U.S. dollar bonds provided a small incremental return advantage over U.S. dollar bonds, but at a considerably higher level of risk. Both categories of fixed income assets outperformed the S&P 500 Index measure of U.S. equity results in both risk and return terms, certainly an unexpected outcome (with its roots in the disastrous 1973-74 results for U.S. equities). Within the equity area, non-U.S. stocks, as represented by the EAFE Index, outperformed U.S. stocks by a considerable margin at only slightly more risk. In contrast to U.S. equities, this asset category performed as it should relative to fixed income assets, providing more return for the higher risk involved.

Concerning the Account Performance Index, its position on the graph reveals an aggregate outcome that is superior to the sum of its component parts. To some extent, but not entirely, this is due to the beneficial effect on performance available from multi-market diversification and the differential covariances involved. In this case, the portfolio manager(s) (apparently) achieved an on-balance positive alpha, adding to total portfolio return by their actions. The inclusion of international (i.e., non-U.S.) securities to a portfolio that would otherwise have held only domestic (U.S.) securities clearly worked to the advantage of this fund over this time period.

9. a. We exchange $1 million for foreign currency at the current exchange rate and sell forward the amount of currency we will accumulate 90 days from now. For the yen investment, we initially receive 133.05 million yen, invest it for 90 days to accumulate 133.05 x (1 + .076/4) = 135.578 million yen (since money market interest rates are quoted as annual percentage rates). If we sell this number of yen forward at the forward exchange rate of 133.47 yen per dollar, we will end up with 135.578 million/133.47 = $1.0158 million, for a 90-day dollar interest rate of 1.58%.

Similarly, the dollar proceeds from the deutschemark investment will be

$1 million x 1.5260 x [1 + (.086/4)] / 1.5348 = $1.0156 million which results in a dollar rate of return of 1.56%, almost identical to that in the yen investment.

b. This is an example of covered interest arbitrage or interest rate parity, which states that the return available in any perfectly hedged transaction must be nearly identical (up to transaction costs) and equal to the risk-free interest rate.

c. We conclude that the 90-day U.S. interest rate is about 1.57%, or 6.28% on an annualized basis.

10. a. The market value of equity of each firm increases by $10 million. Outstanding equity of the two firms is now $220 million.

b. Firm ABC balance sheet before the issue and purchase is

Assets		Liabilities and net worth	
Plant,equipment, etc.	$100 million	Stockholders' equity	$100 million

After the issue of stock and purchase of shares of firm XYZ, the balance sheet is

Assets		Liabilities and net worth	
Plant,equipment, etc.	$100 million	Stockholders' equity	$110 million
Shares in firm XYZ	10 million		

The results for firm XYZ are identical.

d. The weights in both firms would increase since the S&P 500 is a value-weighted index and the market capitalization of each firm is now higher.

CHAPTER 27: MANAGING CLIENT PORTFOLIOS

1. a. An appropriate investment policy statement for the endowment fund
      will be organized around the following major, specific aspects of
      the situation:
      1.   The primacy of the current income requirement;
      2.   The inability to accept significant risk as to 85% of the
           original capital;
      3.   The 10-year time horizon present within the fund's infinite
           life span;
      4.   The unique and dominating circumstance represented by the
           June 30, 1998, capital payout requirement; and
      5.   The requirements of the "spending rule".

      VIZ:
      "The endowment fund's investment assets shall be managed in a
      Prudent Man context to provide a total return of at least 8% per
      year, including an original $500,000 (5%) current income
      component growing at 3% annually. Meeting this current income
      goal is the primary return objective. Inasmuch as $8,500,000 of
      capital must be distributed in cash on June 30, 1998, no
      significant risk can be taken on whatever sum is required to
      guarantee this payout; a normal risk capacity shall be assumed
      with respect to remaining investment assets. The fund's horizon
      is very long term as to assets not required for the 1998
      distribution. The Investment Committee's 'spending rule' shall
      be taken into account in determining investment strategy and
      annual income distributions."

   b. The account circumstances will affect the initial asset
      allocation in the following major ways:
      1.   The aggregate portfolio will have much larger than normal
           holdings of U.S. Treasury and Treasury-related securities.
           Maximum use of discount Treasuries and related zero-coupon
           securities will be made to minimize the risk and the amount
           of total assets that must be "frozen" in order to assure the
           availability of $8,500,000 on June 30, 1998.
      2.   The aggregate portfolio will have much smaller than normal
           holdings of equity securities, given the need to "lock up"
           the 1998 distribution requirement in virtually riskless
           form. The initial mix here might well be 15% zeros, 55%
           discount Treasuries, and only 30% equities; in a normal
           situation, 60-70% in equities would not be uncommon.
      3.   The equity portfolio will emphasize a growth orientation.
           Excess income over the current income requirement will be
           added to equity. Not only must building of future value and
           income come from the rather small equity component of the
           portfolio, but it must also serve an inflation protection
           need as well. Since it does not appear that meeting the
           annual current income target will be difficult initially,

there is plenty of room for lower-yielding issues to be included in the equity mix.
4. The aggregate portfolio risk level will be well below average. The 1998 payout requirement dictates a zero risk posture on a large part of the total, while the Prudent Man environment will act to prevent overzealous risk-taking in the "remainder" portion.
5. The fund's tax exempt status maximizes allocation flexibility, both as to income aspects and as to planning for future capital growth.
6. A 10-year horizon must be accommodated as to a major portion of total capital funds, while a very long term horizon applies to the rest.

2. a. Liquidity

3. b. Employees

4. b. Organizing the management process itself.

5. d. high income bond fund

6. a. An approach to asset allocation that GSS could use is the one detailed in the chapter. It consists of the following steps:
   1. Specification of the asset classes to be included in the portfolio. The major classes usually considered are:
      . Money market instruments (usually called cash)
      . Fixed income securities (usually called bonds)
      . Stocks
      . Real estate
      . Precious metals
      . Other
   2. Specify capital market expectations. This step consists of using both historical data and economic analysis to determine your expectations of future rates of return over the relevant holding period on the assets to be considered for inclusion in the portfolio.
   3. Derive the efficient portfolio frontier. This step consists of finding portfolios that achieve the maximum expected return for any given degree of risk.
   4. Find the optimal asset mix. This step consists of selecting the efficient portfolio that best meets your risk and return objectives while satisfying the constraints you face.

   b. A guardian investor typically is an individual who wishes to preserve the purchasing power of his assets. Extreme guardians would be exclusively in AAA short term credits. GSS should first determine how long the time horizon is and how high the return expectations are. Assuming a long horizon and 8-10% return (pretax) expectations, the portfolio could be allocated 30-40% bonds, 30-40% stocks, and modest allocations to the other asset groups.

7. Investor Objectives:

Return Requirements-- Often the return is stated in terms of minimum levels to fund a specific liability or budget requirements as indicated by the Wood Museum Treasurer. The minimum returns to meet budget are: 1982 - 12%; 1983 - 13%; and 1984 - 14%. The trustees would have to clarify how capital gains should be treated relative to the budget.

Risk Tolerance--the client's willingness or ability to bear risk in the pursuit of specified return requirements. For Wood Museum, the tight budget position and the trustees' fears of a financial crisis indicate a low tolerance for risk.

Investor Constraints:

Liquidity Requirements-- the client's need for cash or cash availability from securities that can be sold quickly and without substantial price risk (concession). Wood Museum's liquidity needs are a significant factor given the budget considerations.

Time Horizon-- the client's expected holding period, which is generally determined by such factors as the nature of the client's liabilities, cash flow requirements or expectations. Investment managers also have an expectational time horizon, which is the distance into the future that the manager feels he can predict earnings, dividends, etc, with reasonable accuracy. For Wood Museum, the immediacy of their budget requirements (1-3 years) suggests a very short time horizon for at least a major portion of the portfolio.

Tax Considerations--Wood Museum is tax exempt.

Regulatory and Legal Considerations--In the case of an endowment fund, prudent man factors must be considered as well as the legal structure of the fund and any state or federal regulation that might influence the management of the investment portfolio.

Unique Needs and Circumstances--particular conditions or requirements that reflect the discretion of the fund trustees. For example, social factors might be a concern of the Museum that the trustees want reflected in the types of investment deemed appropriate for the fund.

8. The most important area of change concerns taxes. Mrs. Atkins pays taxes, but the endowment fund will be free of taxes.

OBJECTIVES

Return Requirement: The fund should strive to provide a predictable stream of income growing in line with inflation. An initial income target of 5% of portfolio assets should enable the fund to support the hospital's operating budget, while still favoring future growth.

Risk Tolerance: In view of the relatively long time horizon, limited liquidity needs, and adequacy of already existing endowment assets to offset the operating deficit, the Atkins Fund has an above average ability to assume risk.

CONSTRAINTS

Liquidity: Liquidity needs are low. Except for investment reasons and periodic payment of accumulated income, there is no reason to maintain any sizable liquid reserves in the fund.

Time Horizon: Endowment funds typically have very long time horizons and there is no reason to believe that the current case is any exception. Certainly the time horizon extends well beyond normal market cycles.

Tax Considerations: Since endowment funds are normally free from taxes, with the exception of minimal estate taxes, this would not be a meaningful constraint for this fund.

Legal: Most endowment funds are governed by state regulations, and since most states have moved to a "prudent man" standard, regulatory and legal constraints should not be significant investment factors (certainly no more so than when Mrs. Atkins was alive).

Unique Needs: Although the details provided concerning Good Samaritan are somewhat sketchy, and additional information might be appropriately requested, it would appear that this hospital is experiencing the financial difficulties which have been characteristic of this industry for several years. The existence of an operating deficit, and the possibility that this deficit may grow, suggest that a slightly more conservative posture relative to other endowment funds might be appropriate.

9. a. Investment objectives are goals; constraints are the limits within which the responsible party may operate to achieve the objectives; policies define the ways in which the effort to achieve the objectives will be undertaken.

The primary function of an **investment objective** is to identify the risk/return relationship sought for an account. Emphasis may be on minimizing risk while obtaining a specific attainable rate of return or on maximizing return while accepting an appropriate level of risk. Objectives may be specified in either absolute or relative form. For example: "8% total return while experiencing a risk level equivalent to the S&P 500" or " a target total return of 3% per annum greater than the rate of inflation with a standard deviation no greater than that of the S&P 500 in the post World War III period."

Investment constraint is a limitation on the investment decision-making which can be identified as liquidity, time horizon, tax consideration, legal or regulatory considerations and unique needs. The realism of both the investment objectives and the practical policies adopted for managing the account must be tested against any investment constraints. For example: an investment advisor to an ERISA plan is legally constrained by virtue of inclusion as a fiduciary under the law and cannot purchase for the plan portfolio over 10% of the common stock of the plan sponsor.

Investment policy is an operational statement or guideline which specifies the actions to be taken to achieve the investment objective within the constraints imposed.

b.   OBJECTIVES

Return: Total return equal to or greater than the spending rate of 5% plus the rate of inflation in medical school tuition.

Risk Tolerance: Moderate -- no less volatility than long-term bonds or more than a diversified portfolio of common stocks.

CONSTRAINTS

Time Horizon: Long-term (Perpetuity)

Liquidity: Modest percentage (5-10%) of assets must be available for annual distribution.

Legal and Regulatory: State regulation and/or the endowment documents.

Taxes: none.

c.   Investment policies.

A portfolio balance, to be averaged over time, of a maximum position of 67% in equity-type investments and a minimum position of 33% in fixed income type investments.

Qualified equity and fixed income investments to consist of the following:

Equity Related	Fixed Income
Common stocks and warrants	Government and agency
Convertible securities	obligations
Option writing	Corporate obligations
	Real estate mortgages
	Private placements
	Security lending programs

In the case of convertible securities, corporate obligations and preferred stocks carrying a credit rating, qualifying for purchase are such securities rated no less than BBB ("regarded as having an adequate capacity to pay interest/dividends and repay principal") as defined by S&P, or its equivalent as defined by other recognized rating agencies. Stocks to be of high quality with betas not to exceed 1.2 for portfolio as a whole.

The Office of the Treasurer to have direct responsibility for no more than 50% of total marketable endowment funds. Remaining fund to be the responsibility of outside managers as selected from time-to-time. All managers to have full investment discretion within defined statements of objectives and policies.
Must distribute minimum of 5% of assets annually as a charitable foundation in order to avoid loss of tax-exempt status.
Sufficient funds available for annual disbursement. Money market instruments rated A-1 may be utilized for a liquidity reserve.

10. Note that the parameters given in this problem are the same as in Table 5 in the chapter with the exception of the expected return on real estate, which has been raised to 11% from 10%.

Effect of changing the $E(r)$ on real estate:

$E(r_r)$ =	10%	11%
Portfolio Proportions		
Stocks	35.02%	33.26%
Bonds	43.43	41.17
Real Estate	21.55	25.57
Parameters of O* portfolio		
$E(r*)$	10.97%	11.17%
$\sigma*$	10.35	10.29
b* (Reward-to-variability ratio)	.480	.502

CHAPTER 28:   MANAGING RETIREMENT ASSETS AND PENSION FUNDS

1. I would advise them to exploit all available retirement tax shelters,
   like 403b, 401k, Keogh plans, IRAs, etc. Since they will not be taxed
   on the interest earned on these accounts until they withdraw the
   funds, they should avoid investing in tax-preferred instruments like
   municipal bonds.
   If they are very risk-averse, they should consider investing a large
   proportion of their funds in inflation-indexed CDs, which offer a
   riskless real rate of return.

2. C.B. SNOW'S WIDOW
   a.   Income:

   (An item marked REAL is expected to increase at the rate of
   inflation. An item marked NOMINAL is expected to remain fixed.)

   Income from Trust Assets:

	Pre-tax	After-tax
Money market fund ($75,000x14.7%) (NOMINAL)	$11,025	$ 7,718
Munis ($105,000x8%) (NOMINAL)	8,400	8,400
Highway Cartage common ($120,000x7.9%)(REAL)	9,480	6,636
Total income from Trust assets	28,905	22,754
Social Security ($600 per mo x 12) (REAL)	7,200	6,120
(Tax on Soc. Sec. = .15x$7,200)		
Total Income	36,105	28,874

Expenses:

Household (REAL)	19,600
Mortgage on new second home ($45,000 @ 17.5%) (NOMINAL)	7,938*
Country Club dues ($125 per mo x 12)(REAL)	1,500
Total Expenses	29,038

*Interest tax savings will be used to pay maintenance fee.

Conclusion:

Her requirements cannot be met for this year without selling some
assets. Furthermore, inflation will cause her expenses, which
are $21,100 REAL plus $7,938 NOMINAL, to increase more rapidly
than her after-tax income, which is $12,756 REAL plus $16,118
NOMINAL.

   b.   Mrs. Snow's objectives seem to be :
        1.   To maintain her current standard of living.
        2.   To leave as much of her assets as possible for her
             daughter, subject to the first objective being met.

c.   Mrs. Snow should use $45,000 of the $300,000 Trust to pay off her mortgage immediately since the after-tax rate of interest on the mortgage of 12.25% per year (.7x17.5%) exceeds what she could earn on alternative fixed-income investments. With no mortgage payment to make, her required real after-tax income would be $21,100 per year.
Her Social Security income is $7,200 per year. By investing all of her remaining $255,000 in low coupon municipal bonds, she could avoid paying any income taxes on her Social Security benefits and maintain the real value of her Trust assets for her daughter. The current yield on the munis would have to be sufficient to cover the difference between her needs of $21,100 per year and her Social Security benefits of $7,200 per year, i.e., $13,900 per year. This implies a current yield of 5.45% per year (13,900/255,000).

3. a.   George More's accumulation at age 65:

	n	i	PV	FV	PMT	
TIAA	25	3	100,000	?	1,500	FV = $264,067
CREF	25	6	100,000	?	1,500	FV = $511,484

b.   Expected retirement annuity:

	n	i	PV	FV	PMT	
TIAA	15	3	264,067	0	?	PMT = $22,120
CREF	15	6	511,484	0	?	PMT = $52,664

c.   In order to get a TIAA annuity of $30,000 per year his accumulation at age 65 would have to be:

n	i	PV	FV	PMT	
15	3	?	0	30,000	PV = 358,138

His annual contribution would have to be:

n	i	PV	FV	PMT	
25	3	100,000	-358,138	?	PMT = $4,080

This is an increase of $2,580 per year over his current contribution of $1,500 per year.

4. a.   Joe's accrued benefit is currently $18,000 per year starting at age 65: .015 x 30 x $40,000.

Its PV at age 65 is $18,000(PA,8%,15) = $154,071, and its PV at age 60 is $104,858.

b.   An actuarially fair annuity starting one year from now would be: $104,858(AP,8%,20) = $10,680 per year.

5. a. A policy statement for the Mid-South Pension Plan would include the following:

OBJECTIVES
(1) The return requirement is at least equal to the actuarial assumption of 7% per year. A return in excess of 7% may be used to reduce Company contributions or increase employee benefits.
(2) The Company on balance has the flexibility to have an average/above average degree of risk. Key factors to consider in reaching this conclusion regarding risk tolerance are:
    a. A defined benefit plan must meet ERISA requirements. ERISA clearly established that only the entire portfolio must meet prudent man responsibilities, not a single security.
    b. The two key actuarial assumptions with regard to return and salary progression are relatively conservative. The rate return assumption of 7% is reasonable relative to historic results of 10%. A salary progression rate of 5% is in line with past results.
    c. The plan is valued on a four-year rolling average. This is a relatively conservative approach.
    d. Mid-South's average employee age is relatively low, and its time horizon long, allowing the plan to take above average risk.
    e. Mid-South's operating results have not been particularly cyclical.
    f. One aspect of the plan would require a more conservative approach. Past service liabilities are relatively high and are to be amortized over a 35 year period of time. This is a liberal approach toward funding past service liabilities.

CONSTRAINTS
(1) The Company's liquidity requirements are about average. Income is required to meet payments to retirees, but contributions are available for longer term investments.
(2) The Company's time horizon is relatively long. It is certainly longer than the normal market cycle.
(3) Tax considerations are not a meaningful constraint. Both contributions and earnings are exempt from taxes.
(4) Regulatory and legal considerations are relatively minor. The plan is subject to ERISA. The prudent expert rule applies to the total portfolio and the plan cannot hold more than 10% of its own stock.
(5) The plan has no particular unique needs except for Mr. Oliver's desire to have the plan serve as a profit center actively managed to maximize return for a given level of risk.

Asset Allocation:

Probability Distribution of Annualized Rates of Return

		Annualized Rate of Return		
Scenario	Probability	Bills	Stocks	Bonds
Cont'd Prosperity	.6	6%	12%	8%
High Inflation	.25	10	15	3
Deflation/Depression	.15	2	-6	12
Expected Return (Mean)		6.40%	10.05%	7.35%
Standard Deviation		2.50	6.86	2.87

Correlation Matrix:

	Bills	Stocks	Bonds
Bills	1.0	.851	-.996
Stocks		1.0	-.804

The strong negative correlation between bill and bond returns makes it possible to eliminate virtually all risk by creating a portfolio consisting of half bonds and half bills (a.k.a. cash). The optimal combination of bonds and stocks to combine with the risk-free portfolio is then 32% stocks and 68% bonds.

PORTFOLIOS:

Probability Distribution of Portfolio Rates of Return

		Annualized Rate of Return	
		Half bills	1/3 stocks
Scenario	Probability	Half bonds	2/3 bonds
Cont'd Prosperity	.6	7%	9.33%
High Inflation	.25	6.5	7.0
Deflation/Depression	.15	7	6.0
Expected Return (Mean)		6.875%	8.25%
Standard Deviation		0.22	1.36

Figure 1 displays the efficient portfolio frontier.

Figure 1. The Risk-Reward Trade Off for Portfolios of Stocks,
              Bonds and Cash

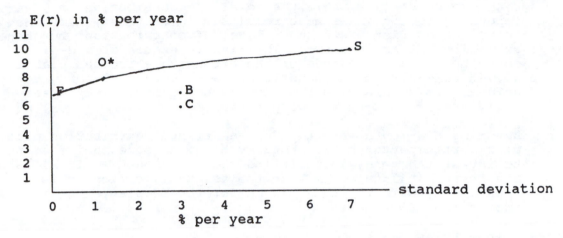

Point F represents a portfolio that is 50% invested in cash and
50% in bonds. It is virtually risk free and offers an expected
return of 6.875% per year. Point B is 100% in bonds, and point S
100% in stocks. Point O* is the optimal combination of stocks
and bonds (32% stocks and 68% bonds) to be combined with the
risk-free portfolio to form the investor's final portfolio. It
has an expected return of 8.2% and a standard deviation of 1.3%.
All efficient portfolios lie along the straight line connecting
points F and O*. The slope of this efficient frontier, the
reward to variability ratio, is:

$$b* = \frac{E(r*)-r_f}{\sigma*} = \frac{8.2\%-6.875\%}{1.3\%} = 1.02$$

To the right of point O*, the efficient frontier is the line
segment connecting points O* and S. It is slightly curved and
relatively flat and represents the risk-reward trade-off
attainable by shifting out of bonds and into stocks. If we
approximate it with a straight line the reward to variability
ratio we get for this segment of the trade-off line is only:

$$b = \frac{10.05\%-8.2\%}{6.86\%-1.3\%} = .33$$

Mid-South should probably hold the O* portfolio. It offers low
risk and an expected return in excess of the 7% actuarial
assumption.

b.   A defined benefit (DB) plan and a defined contribution (DC) plan
     differ primarily in the areas of funding, benefits, and risk-
     bearing focus. A defined benefit plan has a known level of
     retirement benefits while the level of contributions may vary
     depending on the investment results. In contrast, a defined
     contribution plan has a known level of contributions but benefits
     at retirement are unknown. The risk tolerance of a defined
     contribution plan depends on the extent to which the plan is
     viewed as a retirement benefit or as an estate planning tool;
     however, in such a plan the risk is borne by the employees
     individually, not by the corporation.

     Assuming Mid-South were to adopt a defined contribution plan, the
     plan participants should probably be given some choice as to how
     to invest the money in their individual accounts. If Mid-South
     has responsibility for making the asset allocation decision, it
     should stay with the same mix as for the DB plan, that is, 32%
     stocks and 68% bonds.

6. Morgan Industries.
     The firm's outstanding debt is $600 million. Since debt is 35%
     of total capital, the total capital must be $1,714 million
     ($600/.35).   Its corporate and pension fund balance sheets are as
     follows:

Morgan Industries Corporate Balance Sheet
($ millions)

Assets	$1,714	Debt	$600
		Equity	$1,114

Pension Fund Balance Sheet
($ millions)

Stocks	$500	Present Value of	
Bonds	$500	Accrued Benefits	$1,500
		Fund Balance	-500

The combined net worth is $1,114 - $500 = $614 million.
This should presumably be the market value of the company's
shares provided that the book value of the assets and the debt
equal their market values.

According to Black and Dewhurst the market value of the firm's
equity could be increased by $340 million (.34 x $1 billion) as
follows:
1.   Switch the stocks from the pension fund to corporate
     account.
2.   Issue $1 billion of bonds and use the money to invest in
     bonds on pension fund account. $500 million would be to
     replace the stocks, and the other $500 million would be to
     fund the unfunded pension liability.

7. a. The significant differences among the three individuals are rather vividly identifiable via the matrix below:

Investment Considerations	Tom	Margaret	Glenn
Stage in investor life cycle	Late	Early	Middle
Investor Objectives: Return Requirement	High income	High growth	Income and growth
Risk Tolerance	Low; needs stability and/or safety of principal	High; can tolerate volatility	Moderate; needs income/growth balance
Constraints: Liquidity Needs	Marked	None	None
Time Horizon	Limited: 4 years	Very long	Long
Regulatory & Legal	◄--------	Not a factor	-----------►
Tax	◄--------	Plan represents a tax-free environment for all 3	-----------►
Unique Circumstances	Goal of early retirement; large existing asset base	Youth; no family or related constraints	Single parent; family needs

The differences translate into discussion comments as follows:

Re: Tom His goal is to maximize the production of income within the plan account at a low level of risk that promotes stability of principal. The dominant fact relating to his investment situation is his age and his intention to retire early. The resulting fixed four-year horizon virtually dictates an investment approach that's low-risk, liquid and minimizes down-side fluctuation. He enjoys a very clean personal situation, with a second income, a paid-for home and a growth-stock portfolio. His tax rate on non-plan income is probably quite high (vs. a zero rate in the plan), so "outside" is the place to hold low-yielding and growth-oriented assets and "inside" (that is, under the plan) is the place hold yield-oriented assets where income can compound tax-free. Given his fixed horizon for investment under the plan, his low risk tolerance, the size of his total assets, and the fact that other sources of retirement income will be available (investment income and later Social Security), "growth" is simply not a goal. He is in an ideal position to sit back and enjoy the tax-free compounding of income on minimum-risk investment combinations. He is late in his life cycle and there is no need to reach for large returns at the cost of higher risk.

Re: Margaret Her goal will reflect her youth and apparent capacity to assume an aggressive risk posture. With no liquidity needs, a long time horizon, and the plan's tax-free environment, she will probably want to take maximum advantage of the estate-building opportunity present here. Not only is the tax shelter attractive, but she is probably not saving much outside the plan and this means of "forced saving" is probably important. She will have plenty of opportunity to change her asset mix to nail down gains as they occur and/or to protect against adversity as she is early in her life cycle and enjoys a high degree of flexibility under the plan. That flexibility and her long time horizon should be aggressively exploited within the limits of her (probably high) risk tolerance.

Re: Glenn On the one hand, Glenn is relatively young, has a large part of his career still ahead of him. On the other hand, he is not all that far from the heavy expenses associated with teenagers, college, etc. Moreover, he is probably pressed for current cash, given existing circumstances. An approach that balances income production and capital growth in a context of average (or slightly below average risk-taking over an extended horizon is indicated. While no specific constraints are noted, prudent management would appear to favor above average liquidity and below average volatility. Growth of capital is important, but so is protection of the basic investment pool, and this should probably have first priority given the fact of family and the limited outside assets.

b. Tom: Here an allocation of
    .   65% money market fund
    .   15% high-grade bond fund
    .   10% index stock fund
    .   10% real estate fund
    would appear to be a reasonable one for this short horizon,
    liquidity-oriented situation. The 80% in fixed-income form is
    expected to produce a high level of both income and compounding
    with minimal principal instability; the 20% in equity form is
    primarily for diversification purposes but should also contribute
    to income without being a destabilizing factor. The focus is
    minimum fluctuation in the context of a relatively short time
    horizon. The non-residential real estate commitment **complements**
    his "outside" house ownership. The general stock allocation
    complements his "outside" growth stock holdings.

    Margaret: With a focus on long time horizon and ability to take an
    aggressive posture with respect to risk, an allocation of:
    .   40% growth stock fund
    .   30% index stock fund
    .   15% real estate fund
    .   10% high-grade bond fund
    .   5% money market fund
    would appear to be appropriate. The index fund provides broad
    diversification across the equity asset class, while the growth
    fund provides exposure to positive alpha production within it.
    The real estate fund, supplementing her outside condo holding, is
    primarily for exposure of a different equity type and for
    diversification. The 15% in fixed-income form is there for the
    important diversification it provides and for the compounding of
    certain cash flow. As time passes and market conditions and
    estimates change, one would, of course, be considering new mixes
    each six months.

    Glenn: Here the focus is on "middle-of-the-road" aspects: moderate
    return,   longish horizon, and preservation along with enhancement. A
             reasonable allocation would be:
    .   10% money market fund
    .   25% high-grade bond fund
    .   35% index fund
    .   15% growth stock fund
    .   15% real estate fund
    to obtain maximum diversification, liquidity, some emphasis on
    equity but not a concentration, and prospects for good income
    production. If a larger capacity for risk-bearing was perceived,
    the index/growth stock percentages could be reversed as a first
    step, then the fixed-income/equity percentage allocations could
    be changed in favor of equities if appropriate.

In summary, here are the allocations for each of the 3 individuals:

Fund	Tom	Margaret	Glenn
Money market	65%	5%	10%
Bonds	15	10	25
Stock index	10	30	35
Growth	0	40	15
Real estate	10	15	15

CHAPTER 29: MANAGING INVESTMENT COMPANIES

Problems 1-10 were solved on a Lotus 1-2-3 spreadsheet.

1. The market portfolio and T-bill data for quarters 1-10 (when first converted to quarterly rates) yield a quarterly average excess rate of return and standard deviation of (see also Table P2):

    $$r_M = 1.15\% \quad ; \quad \sigma_M = 4.09\%$$

2. First convert the annualized macro forecasts to quarterly rates of return. Then, by subtracting the long run average excess return and the risk-free rate, the forecasts can be represented as predicted deviations from the long-run mean excess return. These predictions are shown in Table Pl. Next to the column of forecasts (s_M) we show the actual market portfolio quarterly deviations of excess returns from the long-run mean (e_M). The statistics at the bottom of the table and the third column which shows the adjusted forecast (s^*) will be used in the next problems.

Table Pl

Quarter	s_M	e_M	s^*_M
1	12.09	2.35	3.68
2	- 6.82	- 6.72	- 2.07
3	3.69	2.96	1.12
4	3.17	5.66	.96
5	- 9.33	3.10	- 2.84
6	-10.94	- 4.25	- 3.33
7	- 2.90	- 1.30	-.88
8	8.82	.67	2.68
9	8.62	3.43	2.62
10	- 2.23	- 5.89	-.68
Average	.42	.00	.13
SD	7.66	4.09	2.33
R-SQR		.3041	

3. To obtain the stock residuals we first compute the stock quarterly excess returns and then regress them against the market's. The stock quarterly excess returns can be computed from the dividend-adjusted prices. Using the beta from the estimated SCL we can compute the expected stock returns, conditional on the market's. Subtracting this expected rate from the actual, yields the stock residual. The intermediate steps for stock A are shown in Table P2. Only the residuals for stock B are shown in Table P2.

Quarter	$r_M - r_f$	$r_A - r_f$	$E(r_A|r_M) - r_f)$	e_A	e_B
1	3.49	1.55	-.08	1.63	-19.11
2	- 5.57	-18.18	.13	-18.31	- 1.10
3	4.10	-47.25	-.10	-47.15	-47.44
4	6.81	-13.85	.16	-13.68	54.16
5	4.24	46.05	-.10	46.15	10.01
6	- 3.10	26.73	.07	26.65	-28.71
7	- .15	-35.80	.00	-35.80	31.24
8	1.82	-25.87	-.04	-25.83	85.12
9	4.57	9.36	-.11	9.47	-40.43
10	- 4.74	.31	.11	.19	27.22
Average	1.15	- 5.70	- .03	- 5.67	7.10
SD	4.09	27.03	.10	27.03	40.70
Beta				- .02	2.60

4. In converting the micro forecasts of stock prices to forecasts of stock return residuals, we have to decide whether to use actual market returns or macro forecasts. Operationally, only the market forecast is known at the time that the micro forecast is constructed. Hence, for the purpose of constructing the optimal portfolio, the macro forecast has to be used to construct the micro forecast.

First we compute the internal rate of return (IRR) that is reflected in the stock price forecasts. From the IRR we subtract the stock rate of return that is expected from the SML. The latter is obtained by applying the stock beta to the macro forecast of the market excess return and adding the risk-free rate. The macro forecasts have to be adjusted in order to make them operationally useful. A simple adjustment is achieved from the regression of the forecasts, s_M, on the residuals, e_M. For the given data on the 10 quarters the regression shows:

intercept = .42% :   R-SQR = .3041 ;   slope = 1.03 ;

These results show no significant bias in the forecast, and hence the simple adjustment technique amounts to down scaling the forecasts using R-SQR. The adjusted forecasts appear in the table Pl. Note that here, for lack of previous observations, we used data of all ten quarters to adjust forecasts that had been made before all these data were actually revealed. In reality, the Evaluation and Attribution Group will be able to use only past date in making these adjustments. The micro forecast for stocks A and B appear in Table P3.

Quarter	IRR_A	$E(r_A - r_f | s_M)^*$	s_A	s_B
1	-11.35	- .12	-12.19	-32.67
2	-28.65	.02	-30.36	34.05
3	-58.58	- .05	-60.47	62.48
4	27.81	- .05	26.44	67.35
5	78.38	.04	77.09	44.86
6	-19.27	.05	-20.57	-43.26
7	-28.32	- .01	-30.06	30.89
8	8.70	- .09	6-29	62-41
9	53.19	- .09	50.58	-51.13
10	- 8.86	- .01	-12.34	36.28
Average			- .56	21.13
SD			39.30	43.44

5. and 6. We use the first 5 quarters to estimate the regression of micro forecasts on actual residuals in order to adjust the micro forecast of Quarter 6. In the next step we use the first 6 quarters to perform the adjustment to the Quarter 7 forecast, and so on. The results are shown in Table P4. By the simple adjustment technique we first correct for the bias and then for accuracy. The correction is done by:

$$s^* = R\text{-}SQR(s - intercept)/slope.$$

The risk involved in the forecast is given by

$$\sigma_\rho^2(e) = (1 - \rho^2)\sigma^2(e)$$

where $\sigma(e)$ is estimated from past stock residuals, and ρ^2 stands for R-SQR.

7. To see what effect, if any, the constraints have, we first solve for the active portfolio weights ignoring the non-negativity and individual-stock maximum-weight constraints. The proportion of an individual stock in the active portfolio is given by:

$$w = \frac{s^*/\sigma^2(e)}{\Sigma s^*/\sigma^2(e)}$$

Table P4

Quarter	Intercept	Slope	R-SQR	s*	$s_\rho^2(e)$
Stock A					
6	8.93	1.41	.82	-17.09	135.11
7	- 2.50	1.08	.55	-14.15	326.39
8	- 1.21	1.03	.57	4.15	315.39
9	2.34	.94	.50	25.43	367.71
10	7.24	1.03	.50	- 9.57	363.67
Stock B					
6	35.44	.33	.09	-22.38	1503.22
7	25.26	.58	.18	1.78	1351.17
8	23.46	.53	.18	13.18	1359.86
9	23.04	.50	.26	-39.11	1222.83
10	16.29	.65	.36	11.23	1053.03

and the proportion of the active portfolio (A) in the optimal risky portfolio (P) is then:

$$w_A = \frac{w_A^*}{1 + (1 - \beta)w_A^*}$$

where w* is the weight that an active portfolio with a beta of 1 would be assigned:

$$w_A^* = \frac{s_A^*/\sigma_\rho^2(e_A)}{(\pi_M + s_M^*)/\sigma_\rho^2(e_M)}$$

and the s_A^*-s_M^* are the adjusted forecasts for the entire active portfolio and the market index

portfolio. The adjusted forecast for the active portfolio residual is the weighted average of the individual stock microforecasts with the optimal proportions of the stocks in the active portfolio as weights. The variances of the market and the active portfolios consist of the estimates of the unconditional rates, adjusted (down scaled) by the ability of the forecasters:

$$\sigma_\rho^2(e) = (1 - \rho^2)\sigma^2(e)$$

Performing the calculations leads to the active portfolio weights and resultant performance forecasts in Table P5.

Table P5

Q	w_A	w_B	S^*_{Active}	$\sigma^2_\rho(e_{Active})$	β_{Active}
6	.8947	.1053	-17.65	124.82	.2522
7	1.0314	-.0314	-14.65	348.51	-.1061
8	.5756	.4244	7.98	349.39	1.0886
9	1.8605	-.8605	80.96	2178.33	-2.2796
10	1.6816	-.6816	-23.75	1517.57	-1.8106

Note that in the absence of constraints, a forecast for negative returns is just as good as a positive one. Second, what appears as extreme positions in the active portfolio will often be moderated by the proportion of the entire active portfolio in the optimal risky portfolio. Finally, the general preference for stock A over B results in part from the better forecasting record of stock A micro forecaster. with characteristics as in Table PS, the weight of the active portfolio in the optimal risky portfolio, and the resultant positions in the individual stocks in the risky portfolio are given in table P6.

Table P6

Quarter	w_{Active}	w_{Index}	w_A (in pf P)	w_B (in pf P)
6	.4837	.5163	.4328	.0509
7	1.7823	-.7823	1.8382	-.0559
8	.0700	.9300	.0403	.0297
9	.0835	.9165	.1554	-.0719
10	4.3124	-3.3124	7.2517	-2.9393

It should be noted that the position of the risky portfolio in the (overall) Complete Portfolio is an integral part of evaluating the effect of the constraints. In the next problem we do just that, so for this problem assume that the optimal risky portfolio is also the complete portfolio. The performance characteristics of portfolio P are:

Table P7

Quarter	Beta(P)	$E(r_p)-r_f$	$o^2(r_p)$
6	.64	- 9.93	33.96
7	-.97	-26.37	1,118.13
8	1.01	4.41	13.53
9	.73	9.50	21.35
10	-11.12	-107.65	29,664.93

The constraints dictate that in <u>quarter 6</u> the risk-free asset should be held. For Quarter 6, the adjusted macro forecast and the micro forecasts for stocks A and B residuals are: -2.18%, -17.09%, -22.38%, respectively. With these forecasts, any superior risky portfolio would call for a short position in one or more of the risky assets. If short positions are prohibited, then the risk-free rate is optimal.

For quarter 7, the macro and two micro forecasts are: .27%, -14.15%, 1.78%, respectively. Without constraints, the active portfolio is constructed so that the optimal risky portfolio (P) will be held short, and thus the resultant positions in the individual assets will be the reverse of what appears in the columns:"w_{Index}," "w_A(in Pf P). and "w_B(in Pf P)" of Table P6. Abiding by the constraint, we have to drop stock A from consideration because it has a negative predicted alpha value. Note that holding a negative alpha (s*) stock in the active portfolio for the purpose of diversification alone is ruled out. That role is already played by stock A in the market portfolio. Treating stock B as a single-security active portfolio we find that the optimal positions would be:

Stock B (now the Active Pf): .0634 ; Index: .9366,

with a performance forecast for the risky portfolio, P, of:

$$\beta_p = [1 + W_B(\beta_B - 1)] = 1.10$$

$$E(r_p) - r_f = \beta_p[E(r_M) - r_f] + w_B s_B^* = 41\%$$

$$\sigma^2(r_p) = \beta_P^2 \sigma_\rho^2(e_M) + w_P^2 \sigma_\rho^2(e_B) = 19.58\%$$

Note that the small position in stock B as an active portfolio results from the large (adjusted) residual variance relative to that of the index portfolio.

For Quarter 8, the optimal position (Table P6) of .93 in the index, .04 in stock A, and .03 in B, is consistent with the constraints.

For Quarter 9, a short position in stock B is called for, because of the forecast of a negative residual (-39.11%). Here, again, because short positions are prohibited, we drop negative alpha stocks (here stock B) and are left with the positive alpha stocks for the active portfolio (here stock A). Computing the optimal position in an active portfolio consisting of stock A we find:

Stock A (now the Active Pf): .1756 ; Index: .8244

with a performance forecast of:

$$E(r_p) = 7.56\% \quad ; \quad o^2(r_p) = 19.19$$

For Quarter 10, the micro forecast for stock A is again negative, and it has to be dropped from the active portfolio. Computing the optimal position in the single-stock (B) active portfolio we find:

Stock B (Active Pf): .4575 ; Index: .5525

with a performance forecast of:

$$\beta_p = 1.730889 \quad ; \quad E(r_p) = 5.95\% \quad ; \quad \sigma(r_p) = 255.37$$

The suggested position of .4575 violates the 25% constraint, however, and hence the position in stock B is set to 25% with the resultant performance forecast for the optimal risky portfolio:

$$\beta_p = 1.40 \quad ; \quad E(r_p) = 3.47\% \quad ; \quad \sigma(r_p) = 88.67$$

8. Ignoring the constraints as a first step, we compute the optimal position in P (the remainder to be invested in the risk-free rate) using the data in Table P7 and the complete answer of Problem 7. The optimal proportion of P in the complete portfolio is calculated from:

$$w_p = \frac{E(r_p) - r_f}{A_m \sigma^2(r_p)}$$

where $A_m = 1.5$.

The results are shown in Table P8, where W_f is the weight of the risk-free asset in the complete portfolio, C.

Table P8

Quarter	$w_p(C)$	$w_f(C)$	$w_{Index}(C)$	$w_A(C)$	$w_B(C)$
6	0.	1.	0.	0.	0.
7	.0139	.9861	.0130	0.	.0009
8	.2173	.7937	.2021	.0088	.0065
9	.2626	.7374	.2165	.0461	0.
10	.0261	.9739	.0196	0.	.0065

Table P8 represents a dilemma that many investment managers face, namely, the prospectus (or other reasons) compels them to hold positions that they consider sub optimal, if not downright undesirable. Here we will just point out some central considerations with respect to each of the quarters.

For Quarter 6, all risky assets are undesirable because each is forecast to under perform the risk-free asset. The position with least disutility is to hold the minimum required weight (50%) in the index portfolio where, at least, diversification is appropriate. The remainder 50% is to be held in the money fund.

For quarter 7, the optimal risky portfolio excludes stock A (except for its weight in the index portfolio). With this constraint, the optimal weight in portfolio P (that maximizes Sharpe's measure under the individual stock constraint) should be 1. 3996 only. The portfolio that guarantees the least reduction in utility (relative to 1. 39% in P) depends on the risk aversion of individual clients. Given that these data are unknown and that it would be impossible to construct a desirable portfolio for each level of risk aversion, the second best solution is to up the weight in portfolio P to 50%. This amounts to investing 50% in the risk-free asset, 46.76% in the index, and 3.24% in stock B.

In quarter 8, the unconstrained (both on individual stocks and on the total position in stocks) optimal position in P calls for 21. 73% in stocks. Here, for the same consideration as in Quarter 7, the second best solution is to up the position in P to 50%. This will amount to investing 49.82% in the index, 2.02% in stock A, and 1.50% in stock B.

In Quarter 9, the (second best) solution is similar to that of Quarter 7 . We end up investing 41. 22% in the index and 8 . 78% in stock A.

Similarly, in quarter 10 we invest 37.55% in the index and 12.45% in stock B.

9.   The individual performance evaluation can be assessed along three lines. First we assess the accuracy of the individual macro and micro forecasts for the desired period. Second, we assess the potential contribution of the forecasts to the sharpe measure of the risky portfolio. Finally, one can argue that the constraints that the organization is facing are part and parcel of the environment that individual forecasters operate in. Accordingly, one should measure the contribution of individual forecasts to the Sharpe's measure of the constrained portfolio.

Beginning with the issue of accuracy of the forecast, Table P9 shows the summary statistics from the regressions of forecasts on subsequent realizations with the available data as of the end of quarters 5-10.

Table P9

Quarter	Intercept		Slope		R-SQR	
	Stock A	Stock B	Stock A	Stock B	Stock A	Stock B
5	8.93	35.44	1.41	.33	.82	.09
6	- 2.50	25.26	1.08	.58	.55	.18
7	- 1.21	23.46	1.03	.53	.57	.18
8	2.34	23.04	.94	.50	.50	.26
9	7.25	16.23	1.03	.65	.50	.36
10	5.18	16.50	1.01	.65	.48	.37

The regression statistics keep changing violently from one quarter to the next, because the time series are so short. Ignoring the unreliability of the analysis due to the small size of the data base, it appears that both analysts are valuable forecasters. Micro forecaster A seems to be more valuable. Forecaster B requires substantial bias corrections. A similar analysis can be performed on the macro forecaster's record.

In terms of the contribution of the micro forecasters to the active portfolio, recall that when optimized (absent of constraints), the square of the Sharpe measure of the risky portfolio is incremented by the square of the ratio of alpha to residual standard deviation for the active portfolio, i.e.,

$$\sigma_P^2 = \sigma_M^2 + \frac{S^*_{Active}}{\sigma_\rho(e_{Active})}$$

where SM is the Sharpe measure of the passive strategy (that is the market portfolio). Moreover, the contribution of each stock to the active portfolio square ratio of alpha to residual standard deviation, is given by the stock's own square ratio of alpha to residual standard deviation. These potential contributions of stocks A and B'to the overall Sharpe measure are shown in Table P10. The first panel of Table P10 shows the contribution of each stock to the active portfolio square ratio of alpha to residual standard deviation. The second panel shows the marginal contribution of each stock in terms of the overall Sharpe measure of the optimized (without constraints) risky portfolio.

Table P10

Quarter	Alpha (s*)		Residual SD		Square Ratio $(S^*/\sigma)^2$	
	Stock A	Stock B	Stock A	Stock B	Stock A	Stock B
6	-17.09	-22.38	11.62	38.77	2.16	.33
7	-14.15	1.78	18.07	36.76	.61	.00
8	4.15	13.18	17.76	36.86	.05	.13
9	25.43	-39.18	19.18	34.97	1.76	1.26
10	- 9.57	11.23	19.07	32.45	.25	.12

Quarter	Market Index		Marginal Contribution	
	$E(r_M) - r_f$	S_M	Stock A	Stock B
6	- 2.18	.64	.84	.09
7	.27	.08	.71	.00
8	3.83	1.12	.02	.06
9	3.77	1.10	.48	.33
10	.47	.14	.25	.11

The standard deviation of the market index that should be used for the calculation of the Sharpe measure is $\sigma_\rho(e_M)$ =3.42%. The contributions are, on average, significant and larger for stock A, in part because of the reliability of stock A analyst. An argument can be made that these potential contributions are irrelevant in the face of the constraints that the organization is facing. (The greatest value of an analyst is in an organization that faces no constraints.) Calculation of the marginal contribution to the Sharpe measure of the constrained risky portfolio, in the same way as in Table P10, would show much smaller contributions.

10. The active portfolio performance is assessed on the basis of its contribution to the Sharpe measure of the overall portfolio. Table Pll shows the contributions to the unconstrained active portfolio in quarters 6-10.

Table P11

Quarter	SM	Alpha / Residual Std	Marginal Contribution
6	.6373	1.58	1.07
7	.0783	.78	.71
8	1.1212	.43	.08
9	1.1035	1.73	.95
10	.1378	.61	.49

The quarterly contributions in Table P11 are instructive in three ways. First they show the potential value of active portfolio management. As we said earlier, the ability of the analysts as reflected by the available data is greater than what may be expected in reality. At the same time, however, realistic active portfolios will include many more stocks, consolidating the potential from active management to offset a lesser forecasting ability in the individual stock level. This leads us to the second observation. Compare the contributions in Table P11 to those from individual stocks in Table P10. Broadening the active portfolio to include more stocks is powerful. To the extent that stock residuals are uncorrelated, adding more stocks increments the <u>square</u> of the Sharpe measure, and thus the improvement in the Sharpe measure itself is diminishing. Finally, the value of active management will be decreased by effective constraints on short and long positions.

11. In Problems 9 and 10 we performed the calculus of performance evaluation on the unconstrained portfolio. Here we show an evaluation of the complete portfolio that is based on the constraints. Table P12 shows the expected returns and the Sharpe measure of the passive strategy relative to the constrained complete portfolio. Recall that the position in stocks is constrained to remain in the range of 50%-90%. We shall assume that without active management, the passive portfolio would be invested 70% in the index portfolio and 30% in a money fund.

Table P12

Quarter	Passive (70%) Strategy		Active Complete Portfolio	
	$E(r) - r_f$	S_M	$E(r_c) - r_f$	S_c
6	- 1.53	- .6373	- 1.09	- .6373
7	.197	.0783	.21	.0927
8	2.68	1.1212	2.34	1.1989
9	2.64	1.1035	3.78	1.7258
10	.33	.1378	1.74	.3685

The complete portfolio is shown to be superior to the passive strategy. Note that in Quarter 8, the risk premium on the complete portfolio is smaller, but so its variance and hence the Sharpe measure of the complete portfolio is greater than that of the passive strategy.

12. The main objective of the forecast adjustment process is to convert the raw forecasts to unbiased ones. A by-product of the adjustment process is our ability to perform the entire evaluation of the portfolio management team from the forecast data alone. The adjustment process itself can then be evaluated by testing whether the deviations of portfolio returns

from forecasts are no more than random noise and whether the variance of these deviations is in line with the assessed ability of the forecasters. The available database is too small to support any reliable conclusions. An idea of the potential of this analysis can be obtained from regressing forecasts of the returns on the constrained complete portfolio (as in Table P12) on the actual returns. The results show:

Intercept: -28% ; Slope: .76 ; R-SQR: .78.

These result are satisfactory. (Of course, with a large sample, a slope of this magnitude would be suggestive of bias.) Note in particular the large R-SQR, indicating the combined ability of the three forecasters.

13.   Using the money rates we transform the raw macro forecasts to qualitative forecasts, where "+" stands for a forecast that the market portfolio will outperform the risk-free rate, and "—" otherwise. Using the actual market portfolio returns we denote by "u" a positive excess return, and by "d" otherwise. The forecasts and realizations for the entire 10 quarter period are summarized in Table P13.

Table 13

Quarter	Forecast	Realization	Cumulative:			
			u	d	+"+	-"-
	+	u	1	0	1	0
2	-	d	1	1	1	1
3	+	d	1	2	1	1
4	+	u	2	2	2	1
5	-	u	3	2	2	1
6	-	d	3	3	2	2
7	-	d	3	4	2	3
8	+	u	4	4	3	3
9	+	u	5	4	4	3
10	-	d	5	5	4	4

As a previous comment makes clear, we have on our hands excellent forecasters of quality that one can hardly expect in a nearly efficient market. In that respect, the data and analysis of Problems 1-10 are not sufficiently realistic.

Beginning with quarter 6, the cumulative columns of Table P13 for the end of quarter 5 imply that Pl = 2/3 =.67, and P2 = 1/2 = .5. Hence, $P^* = Pl + P2 - 1 = .67 + .5 - 1 = .17$. (Obviously, this is too small a sample for any far reaching conclusions, but for the sake of the exercise, we ignore the reliability issue here.) At this point, the record shows no ability on the down side, with substantial forecasting ability on the up side. These translate to a value of P^* of .16 which is far from trivial. Using the quarterly standard deviation of the excess return (Table Pl) of 4.09%, and with a switching strategy (between 50% and 90% in stocks) of $\Delta = .9 - .5 = .4$, the per-period potential timing (option) value is:

$$V_q = P^* \Delta_c = .17 \times .4 \times [2N(.5s - .0205) - 1] = .0111.$$

This amounts to a value of 1.11% per dollar invested per quarter (to be deducted as a load at the beginning of the quarter). On an annual basis this amounts to a fair timing load (per annum) of VA $100(1.0111^4 - 1) = 4.51\%$. In a similar way we proceed to compute these values for the balance of the quarters, and present the results in Table P14.

Table P14

Quarter	P	Vq(% per quarter)	VA(% per annum)
6	.17	1.11	4.51
7	.33	2.15	8.86
8	.42	2.73	11.38
9	.50	3.25	13.65
10	.55	3.58	15.09

As Table P14 shows, our macro forecaster, if real, carries a phenomenal value.